CU00970557

DAUGHTERS

by

Helen Hudson

Grosvenor House
Publishing Limited

The right of Helen Hudson to be identified as the author of this
work has been asserted by her in accordance with Section 78
of the Copyright, Designs and Patents Act 1988

The book cover picture is copyright to Inmagine Corp LLC

This book is published by
Grosvenor House Publishing Ltd
28-30 High Street, Guildford, Surrey, GU1 3EL.
www.grosvenorhousepublishing.co.uk

A CIP record for this book
is available from the British Library

ISBN 978-1-78148-847-8

CHAPTER ONE

January the 15th 1958

A baby girl comes into the world in plump and pink perfection. I was named simply Helen Crooks. My parents believed that during a lifetime you would fill out many forms and documents and it was easier to have a short name and one that could not be shortened; for this reason they didn't give me a second name either.

The doctors had warned my mother since she had been four and a half months into her pregnancy that the baby could possibly be brain damaged. Mum and Dad had been in a very serious car smash on their way back from the 1957 Farnborough Air Show. They were returning from the air show in the happy knowledge that they were going to be parents for the first time. Their car was involved in a head-on collision with a lorry. My dad sustained a fractured skull and was given twenty-four hours to live whilst my Mum had a dislocated hip and spent the rest of her pregnancy in plaster. Her bump was showing nicely and the doctors were cutting a little more plaster away to allow me to grow.

I was once shown a picture of the wreckage, it was a miracle anyone got out alive. Friends and family had not been told of the forthcoming happy event as in those days it was normally kept a secret until the bump was showing. Now everyone knew and waited out the rest of the pregnancy in fear of the worst-case scenario.

Somehow by shear determination my dad pulled through those first twenty-four hours. He had to learn to talk again, he had to learn to walk again, he had to learn to read again and he had to learn to write again. Over the next few months he would go on to achieve all of these things and to remember that he was going to be a father quite soon. He told me of the times he went to visit mum in hospital. He would set off from the village where we lived, on the bus, because he was still not allowed to drive. A change of bus in the city would take him out to the hospital. He didn't manage it on more than one occasion because he was thrown off the bus. The bus conductor would assume his slurred speech was due to drunkenness.

How many times have you put someone in a pigeon-hole only to be completely wrong in your assumptions?

Kenneth Henry Crooks made a full recovery but he paid the price with poor health for the rest of his life. He went on to become a kidney patient for over twenty-five years and had two kidney transplants.

Hospitals and hospital visiting would become the family's axis. By the time I was in my late teens I would know my way round several major hospitals. Dad became used to hospital procedures and was an easy-going patient.

Doreen Crooks made a full recovery but suffered with agoraphobia for many months after the accident.

This dramatic and almost catastrophic event in their young lives made them the people they would become, and ultimately, affect the adult I would become.

This single event played a big part in turning them into very controlling parents.

I had loving parents who must have been so grateful that I was a normal little girl. I also had loving maternal and paternal grandmothers. My maternal grandfather died when I was eighteen months old; my paternal grandfather deserted my grandmother and my dad when Dad was only small. My two Nannies were very special to me. Dad's mum I called Gran and mum's mum I called Mam-mam.

Life was good, we were fairly well off; we owned a car and often went out on day trips and we always had a fortnight's holiday in Newquay, Cornwall each year. One trip down to Cornwall when I was two years old I sang *Little Sir Echo* all the way there! I tanned as brown as a berry sleeping peacefully under the canopy of my Silver Cross pram.

Dad was a printer and had courted mum at the local dances where he was pretty surefooted. He was very tall and handsome; when Mum saw him for the first time she thought, "he's the one for me." They did a lot of motorbike riding with another four friends. The six of them on three big bikes would think nothing of a two hundred mile round trip in an evening. This was before the 'mods and the rockers' used to congregate in large numbers at seaside resorts and wreak havoc. Dad would have called it serious biking. Mum was so comfortable as a pillion passenger that she once dropped off to sleep on the back of the bike.

Before having me mum worked for thirteen years as a wages clerk. We lived in a council house, which Dad later went on to buy.

The sixties were dawning and war was thirteen years past. I was an only child for three glorious years before my brother and sister arrived. The twins were born in February 1961. This was another traumatic event in mum and dads lives because they didn't actually know they were expecting twins until they arrived, rendering my dad speechless for four days!

I can still visualise picking the twins up from the maternity hospital. Mum and Dad were proudly sat in the front seat of our Singer Gazelle estate. Number one daughter (me) was on the back seat and in the very back of the estate car were a pink carrycot and a blue carrycot. I remember kneeling up (no seat belts in those days) and looking over into the back to see two swaddled sleeping bundles and thinking to myself, "they can go back as soon as they like".

My sentiments were reiterated when two clucking grandmothers were at home awaiting our return. Suddenly I was a big sister and could fetch and carry and be mummies little helper. Those two grandmothers only had eyes for the new arrivals.

Since having my own children I've realised just how hard it is not to effect sibling rivalry. You try to consider the elder child's feelings but some jealousy always remains. That, I suppose is life.

One spooky fact I learned much later on was that my brother carried the same scar as Mum had from the accident, an injury from the dashboard. I was the one in the womb at the time of the accident!

For this new sister the walks to the next village where Gran lived took on a new meaning. Literally walking, I couldn't sit on the large Silver Cross twin pram Paul and Jayne laid in, head to tail. I would walk alongside and regularly, clumsily fell and badly grazed my knees.

As we grew up, the three of us would get along as well as most siblings can. At the end of the day three will always be an odd number. I was the eldest and bossiest, my sister didn't always want to play girlie things. Jayne was and still is a bit of a tomboy. My brother Paul was an asthmatic child and didn't do rough and tumble boy's stuff so much. The twins sometimes just didn't need anyone else to play with, especially me.

I felt left out because I couldn't occupy as much of my parents time as I once had.

It must have been hard to feed and clothe three pre-school children on one wage but they managed it quite well. Mum was quite adept with a sewing machine and made herself, Jayne and I some of our clothes. The trouble with being same sex we got dressed the same even though we were three years different in age. I remember one year she made us poly-cotton bikinis and beach cover ups. As soon as we went into the sea in our bikinis they shrunk! That was good for me because mine was just right for Jayne and I got to have a bought costume and we weren't dressed alike for once!

*

Soon enough the time came for me, aged five, to go to school; you didn't go to nursery school in those days. I didn't think very much to the idea at all.

Every time the bell rang for morning playtime I would run home, Mum would have to take me back to school. The same thing would happen when the bell rang for lunchtime or afternoon break. I hated the third of a pint of warm sour milk we had each morning during the summer months. Equally nasty was the freezing cold bottle with lumps of ice in it during the winter. There didn't seem to be a time when it was just right but we were forced to drink it anyway.

I am left-handed and I can remember being forced to use my right hand to write with for a short time, this seemed barbaric and it didn't work, I remain a faithful left-hander to this day. I made friends easily and one or two of those primary school friends are still a big part of my life today.

The playground was a cruel place for a bespectacled girl with a name like Crooks. "How many times have you been in the nick, Crooks?" "Four-eyes, four-eyes!"

All through school I found learning moderately easy and good school reports were always rewarded with presents from my parents. My dad always made a big deal about good behaviour and manners and would delight in the rewarding process. Maybe he wasn't sufficiently praised as a child, or the fact that his own father disappeared early in his life made him so generous in his praise and rewards. Dad was always strict and would not hesitate to use his slipper on our backsides if he thought it necessary. Mum would be the one telling us to, "wait till your father gets home".

She would tell him what we had been up to and then we would get it.

She did once lash out at me with a length of washing line I had been skipping with; I'd accidentally caught my sister with it. When Mum saw the large weal she had made on the back of my leg she hugged me and cried with remorse.

In some ways Dad was a bit too strict with us but we always said it didn't do us any real harm. I know that even as an adult I had huge respect for him but was always a little bit scared too.

Weekends were spent in happy pursuit of one of my dad's passions, that of car rallying. We would spend the day motoring through Cambridgeshire or Leicestershire ending up at some disused airfield or another to picnic with fellow rallying people.

I remember one occasion when my parents were having a heated exchange about the route, Father decided he could stand it no longer. He put mum and the three of us out onto the grass verge and drove off at speed. I was the only one to cry; the twins thought it was a good game. Mother on the other hand was too angry to feel anything but anger. He did return a little while later; a little bit calmer and picked us up from a little further down the same stretch of road.

After this, I always imagined my parents were going to abandon us if they went out anywhere. When they went to visit my sick grandmother, leaving an old aunt babysitting, I'd be the one crying, not the twins.

On one occasion they left us all in the car, in the hospital car park while they popped in to see Gran, again it was me sobbing uncontrollably.

My parents' relationship seemed stable enough until something would upset the equilibrium. I often heard heated arguments from my bed but never knew what had started them. Stony silences would go on for days and days after and I was used as the go-between and runner. "Go and tell your dad his dinner is on the table." "Tell your mum I'm not hungry at the moment." Backwards and forwards I would go.

When I was about six or seven my dad had actually packed a bag and was leaving when I was called into their bedroom. I remember being absolutely distraught and sobbing uncontrollably. In the end Dad was in tears too, the upshot was that he didn't leave. I found out when talking to Jayne that she remembers it well too and that we were all asked who we wanted to live with. We all decided we would stay with Mum; this increased the flow of tears to a torrent. We think he had been having an affair but we never knew the details. I never found out what that argument was about and in later years it wasn't mentioned. I've got a feeling they both thought we were too young to have remembered it. There was a culture in the family that if you didn't talk about things, eventually they would go away.

Dad was in the St. John Ambulance Brigade for many years. Being a six-footer he always looked smart in his uniform. He would spend hours polishing his boots, leather belt and the brass buttons on his jacket. He would enjoy putting a razor sharp crease in his own trousers, not allowing mum to do it.

When he was on duty at the pictures he would take me with him, I would sit on my own, enthralled in the film. During the interval an ice cream or some sweets would be passed along the row to me. I would refuse them politely thinking they had come from a stranger! The treat was obviously from Dad.

The annual holiday in Cornwall was particularly memorable in 1965 because both grandmothers came too. The seven of us and our entire luggage was loaded into Dad's beloved car. The journey from Peterborough to Newquay would have taken about twelve hours in those days. What a blissfully happy time, long lazy days on the beach. Gran was already poorly during that holiday, she had leukaemia. The photographs show her wrapped up in several layers of clothing even on the warmest of days. Her party trick of taking out her bottom denture and pulling her lip right up to her nose never failed to amuse me.

In the evenings we would stroll around the town then find somewhere to have a milky drink before heading back to our 'digs'. One particular evening Jayne somehow got separated from the rest of us. Mum and dad were understandably beside themselves because the bed and breakfast place was three busy streets away and Jayne was only four years old. We went straight back there to find my sister safe and well and not realising what all the fuss was about. Until, that is, my father leathered her with his belt. I'm sure it was total relief that made him do it, but still too harsh a punishment for one so young.

The three of us spent a considerable amount of time during that evening aggravating her reddened buttocks with a hairbrush to make the injury look worse, in the naive belief that he would show remorse and never smack any of us again. We were wrong of course.

Dad was an only child brought up by his mother on her own, as mentioned earlier his father had deserted them when Dad was quite young.

Mum was one of four brought up by both parents. Uncle Roy was the eldest followed by Mum; then there was a sister Carole who died aged fourteen and lastly Uncle Maurice. The whole family lived in a three-bedroom house in Eye. Mam-mam and Granddad had married during the depression in 1926. They both worked jolly hard 'on the land' and owned an allotment where they grew vegetables. Working 'on the land' entailed whatever task was needed seasonally for whichever local farmer. Hoeing the fields by hand during the growing season and then helping to bring in the crop at harvest time and all the jobs in between. This was the tail end of the age of the horse! They were easy going folk who just got on with whatever was thrust upon them. I never knew my Uncle Maurice until I was turned seven because he and mum fell out when I was a babe in arms. Apparently mum had changed my nappy in close proximity to the dining table during a family get together. Maurice had taken her to task over it and the resulting rift lasted seven years, with no contact. This sort of thing would reoccur many times over the years with different people. If you didn't sing from the same song sheet as my parents, you were exiled.

Mam-mam was an inexhaustible cake maker; she usually made around 50 Christmas cakes each year for family and friends. The rest of the year and especially in the summer she would make three tier wedding cakes and cater for wedding receptions. She wasn't very enterprising, as she didn't charge very much, she really enjoyed doing it though. As quite a young girl I was roped in to help, my job would be to butter endless rounds of bread for sandwiches. She was a stickler and would inspect my work and give back any slices that needed re-doing. The butter had to be right up to the edge! Sometimes I was allowed to help at the actual reception and found myself serving bottles of brown ale on more than one occasion. There was an awful amount of washing up on these occasions too.

The three of us were allowed pets and had all the usual small rodents. I also remember having a stray cat that would allow me to dress it in doll's clothes and be pushed around in my doll's pram. During school holidays I was allowed to bring home the school pets and any other unclaimed animals that needed looking after.

One particular Christmas holiday I ended up with about a hundred mice, four guinea pigs and six gerbils. They were in various cages stacked in what was once our coal shed, covered down with blankets. That December was extremely bitter and every last animal perished in the severe frost. Mum said, "don't you ever offer to do that again young lady!" Never mind about how dreadful I was feeling at the prospect of returning to school to tell my friends that their beloved pets were dead.

When it was the twins turn to go to school they went more readily than I had done. They had each other for moral support.

Sometimes I got to spend precious time with Mammam, whom I adored. I had a very special relationship with her. We called her Mam-mam because my cousins' Jean and Christine started it and so we carried it on. Jean was five years my senior and Christine was two years older than me. Whenever I went to stay with Mam-mam I had my cousins for company as they lived in the same village.

I remember being snowed in Mam-mam's village, one year, over the Christmas break and not seeing Mum, Dad and Paul and Jayne for several days including Christmas Day and Boxing Day. Years later when I was in exile it was Mam-mam who treated me just the same as she'd always done and firmly refused to be embroiled in the friction between my parents and myself. She didn't take sides either, she stayed firmly neutral.

In 1968 my dear Gran died of leukaemia. She had come to live with us a few months earlier. When she was at the end of her life and bedridden I would sit with her while I knitted dishcloths. Gran would often tell me off for fidgeting; she simply couldn't stand a swaying leg or a tapping foot. When she finally passed away, us kids were sent to relatives out of the way until the doctor had been and the body removed to the chapel of rest. I had never lost anyone close before and didn't know how to grieve, I was ten years old. I felt guilty that I hadn't cried and worried that she would always be able to see me from where she was. She died on Good Friday, would she be like Jesus and come back to us in three days time? That's what I remember thinking at the time. We children didn't attend the funeral, we were considered too young. After the funeral I saw aunts and uncles I'd never seen before. They all swooped in to fight over Grans' belongings. Some of the things that were rightfully my Dad's were taken and never seen again. I witnessed two great-aunts fighting over a fur coat. It ended up with the coat being nearly ripped in half. What a fiasco how stupid could adults be?

Sometimes during the long summer holiday I was shipped off to an old aunt and uncle who lived in Southend-on-Sea. They doted on me, as they had no children of their own. I would spend endless days on the beach and swimming 'like a dolphin' according to Aunt Win. Uncle Frank and Aunt Win would enjoy a drive along the promenade with the windows open, shouting, "wogs go home" to any ethnic minorities that were walking along. I felt it was a bad thing to do this, but what could an impressionable eleven-year-old do about it? I think, as they had both served their country during the war, they perversely thought that they had some sort of right to make racist remarks. I of course didn't know anything about racism until then.

I had a lot of old aunts and uncles because my great grandparents had raised fourteen children.

Thinking back to those years; we visited another old aunt, who lived in the centre of Leicester. When we went to the nearby swing park there, us three Crooks' were the only white children playing there. I can't remember us bothering too much about it but I recall comments from my parents.

My cousin Lynda, who is a year younger than me, and I, once spent a happy week at Aunt Eva's sleeping top to toe in a three-quarter bed. She didn't even mind if we bounced on the bed! While staying there we were introduced to a new fruit; the hairy peach, we had never seen or tasted one before. How exotic was that.

That same cousin looked up to me and I taught her some choice rhymes. "I'm a little nigger girl, I don't swear, shit bugger arsehole, I don't care." Goodness knows where I ever learned it but when my Aunt Audrey, Lynda's mum heard it, was I in trouble!

My dad made my own arse pretty warm I can tell you.

Two years later when I was about twelve and she would have been eleven I taught her how to swing across to the central pole on the 'witch's hat'* and slide down the central pole 'fireman style'. The last time she came to demonstrate this new skill to her younger brother Carl she knocked her two front teeth out.

So she was unfortunate enough to start wearing a plate with two false teeth on at that young age. All thanks to cousin Helen. I did feel dreadful but of course it was too late for recriminations.

---

*A conical roundabout that doubled as a climbing frame. It could be spun round or from side to side at speed.

CHAPTER TWO

1970

Sometimes Mam-mam came to babysit us while my parents went to a dinner dance or a party and she would stay over. She would stay over to help mum nurse dad through a cracking hangover. In those days my dad would come home roaring drunk and spend three or four days on the settee in the lounge. This was quite shocking when I was very young as I thought that he was dying.

The time arrived to take the eleven-plus exam, my parents didn't put any pressure on me, they just knew I would try my best, which I did.

I didn't pass the exam and so my senior school was to be the local comprehensive. Stanground Comprehensive was a very large school with 1,500 pupils, all bigger and more confident than me. There were endless corridors to get lost in but after a very short while it felt more familiar and I settled down to advanced learning. Some of my friends had come up from junior school with me so we were all in the same boat together.

Lessons were enjoyable because we were made to feel quite mature. I enjoyed playing hockey and netball but didn't enjoy cross-country running one bit! We were very fortunate in that there was a large heated swimming pool and I was able to indulge my pleasure of diving and taking part in swimming galas. I particularly liked my maths teacher who was only ten years older than me, it being his first teaching post. I didn't have a crush on him but admired him for his teaching style.

Suddenly maths was no longer an unsolvable riddle but something I could be remotely good at. I'm convinced that the old school maths masters deliberately made the subject seem more difficult to keep the number of people in the fraternity to a minimum.

I was also enjoying learning to speak French. For it's time, the language lab was a state of the art classroom, with cubicles and individual headphones and speakers for one to one learning.

I was fast approaching the dreaded teenage years. I was a terrible teenager, really moody and confrontational. There can't be a worse combination than a premenstrual teenager and a menopausal mother. The clashes were monumental. My dad was still very strict and would say, "you do as I say, not as I do" when I would try to reason or rebel in some way.

Teenagers soon discover that parents and elders are 'cracked vessels'. When you're 13 you only like people who are 13; anyone older is rubbish and anyone younger is stupid. Hormones and boys together are a bad combination.

I no longer wore glasses and had grown tall and leggy. I had thick straight mousey hair almost down to my waist. I didn't think I was beautiful but I was OK to look at.

I absolutely adored David Cassidy and would dream of meeting him and being with him forever. My bedroom walls were covered in posters of him; even to this day I go all gooey at the thought of him. My first real date was with a boy called Trevor Ward; he had sent me a Valentine's card and then invited me to go with him to a football match. It was a Saturday match and the Posh were playing the Canaries. Trevor didn't ask if I liked football nor did he tell me that he was going to be on duty as a St. John Ambulance cadet at the match. I spent the whole game on my own in the stands while Trevor was down at the side of the pitch. This relationship was doomed from the start! My dad dropped me off near the stadium before kick-off and picked me up afterwards, I hadn't even exchanged words with my so-called boyfriend!

There were one or two other trysts at the school youth club but nothing memorable until I met a boy called Glen Simpson. We would meet at the local swing park that teenagers referred to as the rec. (Short for recreation not wreck!) I was allowed out, even after dark in the winter months and the gang would play torch tiggy. The rules of the game were that you had to crawl, commando style, from the perimeter of the rec without being caught in the torch beam. The person who was 'it' sat at the top of the slide scanning right around. If you made it back to the slide without being seen then you had your turn at being 'it.' That was if you were fortunate enough not to have crawled through dog pooh so that no one wanted to be anywhere near you anyway!

There was snogging and a bit of petting but nothing too serious. Back at school girlfriends would compare notes as to how far they'd been with their boyfriends. I'm sure as with teenagers everywhere, they brag about doing more than in truth they really did. We had a number system: 25 was a snog, 50 was a fondle of your boobs, 75 was a finger in your knickers and 100 was all the way. Glen only got as far as 50!

I was very close to one particular girlfriend called Cheryl Fox, we'd been friends since our infants' school days and shared intimate details with each other.

We used to go to her house where we would listen to her mum's LPs of musicals. We would play the records on Cheryl's radiogram in her bedroom while joss sticks fragranced the air. 'Oklahoma' or 'Seven Brides for Seven Brothers' were our favourites and we would sing along gustily. If more of the gang were together we would congregate in my mum's dining room.

When it got close to bonfire night all the lads would go off on sorties to find and chop logs for the rec bonfire. Sometimes they would let the girls go too, I'd be one of the chosen ones wielding an axe. We would chop branches and lug them back to our rec. The pile would get bigger and bigger and sentries would be posted to guard the stack. The boys would get into scraps with other gangs. Each gang would steal the others wood or destroy their bonfire only to have the same done to them in return. You had to hope that by November the fifth you had something left to burn!

This frenzied gang rivalry ended in Glen being carried back to the rec with knife injuries. When I became hysterical, all the boys fell about laughing, as it was all a set up joke. This was too much humiliation to bear. I didn't want him to think I cared too much for him because I didn't. That signalled the end of our relationship. He wasn't particularly handsome and he was very spotty and he wore glasses. He didn't even kiss that nicely either! I came to the decision that our relationship was not going to last if he took enjoyment from my embarrassment.

I decided that Glen's best friend Dave Hudson was better looking, didn't have spots or wear glasses and seemed more my type. So I asked him if he would consider going out with me. His reply was that his loyalty was to his mate and he wouldn't steal his friends' girl.

Well, it all started with Adam and Eve didn't it, and that forbidden fruit? The more Dave didn't seem to want me the more determined I was to have him. I made sure I looked as provocative as a thirteen-year-old could and set about changing his mind. Two days later I asked him out again and this time my magic must have worked because he said yes! The year is 1971. The date is the 16th July. I am thirteen and Dave is fifteen. After a few nights of torch tiggy with the gang and a bit of snogging and fumbling, we were an item. Dave and I settled into a comfortable relationship and enjoyed spending time together. We would walk to and from school together and spend evenings either at my house, in the dining room, or at Dave's house in his front room.

The very first time he took me to his house, only round the corner from mine, he whisked me in through the kitchen where I briefly met his mum, and into the front parlour. On the way I'd glimpsed a man in work clothes, I asked who he was. I was told by Dave, "oh, it's only the lodger."

In the fullness of time I found out it was really his dad. On that first occasion Dave was embarrassed to introduce me to him because he'd just come in from work and was very dirty. Fancy being ashamed of your own father!

Percy worked as a stoker at the nearby brickworks. His job was to keep the fires going inside the huge kilns where the bricks were baked. He was eighteen years older than Dave's mum and as Dave was the youngest of four it meant that he was now an elderly dad, to Dave this was another reason to be embarrassed.

Dave's mum Hilda was an absolute sweetie, a German lady who had married the wartime soldier who patrolled near her house in Germany. She took to me and always wanted to feed me up, as is the German way, she always made me so welcome.

She worked as a silver service waitress at the Angel Hotel in the centre of Peterborough. She did several shifts, cycling each time to the hotel and back. Some days she would do breakfasts, lunches and evening meals and look after the house and the family in between. Of her brood of four, Dave was the youngest and the only one still at home.

The eldest, Margaret was married to Gordon and had two girls, next came Peter who was married to Jenny then came Ronnie who was married to Margaret and lastly Dave.

A lot of our courting was done in that front room where Dave's siblings had done their courting. The sofa bore witness to this with springs sticking out all over the place. Sometimes both Hilda and Percy were out at work, leaving us alone in the house.

Other times we would go to my house and listen to music in my dining room.

We were very shy in the early days and used my old typewriter to communicate our feelings for each other. We would each type a coded message for the other and then set about decoding it together.

SWALK was an easy one; but not one we'd invented ourselves. IWLTKYAO [I would like to kiss you all over] or ITYARL [I think you are really lovely] became easier to unscramble when you got the gist of it.

As we got to know each other better those messages became more X-rated. We were falling more and more desperately in love.

We still spent time with the rest of the gang, Dave and Glen would go fishing with my cousins Steve and Colin or other mates and I spent time in the rec with girlfriends.

One friend, Marie owned a little battery operated, portable record player that played only 45's. We would take it to the rec and play it loudly and sing along with it at the tops of our voices. We would work ourselves up really high on the swings while we sang.

We played favourite '70s music; David Cassidy; Marc Bolan and 10cc and Sweet. I remember one disastrous time when the chain broke on Cheryl's swing leaving her swinging to and fro, taking all the skin off her back.

Sometimes I would take our family pooch along with us, a lovable Alsatian called Ranger; we would throw those 45's like Frisbees for the dog to retrieve. We discovered that they didn't play very well with teeth marks in them!

In the houses that bordered the rec everybody knew everybody. On one side of the rec were people that lived opposite Dave's house and as I only lived a street away there were people who knew my family too. We were being watched!

On one particular occasion we were in the gang doing what teenagers do, minding our own business, when a busybody who overlooked the rec went to report to my parents.

She reported that she had heard bad language being used. Maybe she did, it didn't necessarily mean I was using it. When I got home for my tea my dad was waiting for me on the back doorstep with a bar of lifebuoy soap in his hand. He forced me to eat some of it saying "that will clean up your foul mouth girl "and took the slipper to me for good measure.

I was often in the wrong place at the wrong time. On two occasions when I was younger the police had reason to call at my house. The first time was when my brother and sister, cousins' Linda and Carl, Cheryl and her sister Lorraine and I were out together in a gang. We often used to act out a television programme of the time called *The Monroe's*. We made a den in a field where all the long grass had been recently cut. A rival gang came into the field and proceeded to steal our grass.

We declared war and went home to get our potato guns! We returned to the scene of the crime and a scrap ensued. The other gang went to get their weapons, we followed them home and the scrap continued in the street. Not content with the amount of injuries you could inflict with a potato gun someone threw half a potato and in the melee one of our rivals slipped and broke a wrist. The poor victim's mother called the police and as I was the eldest in the group it was me they called on.

The second time I was out with the gang when an older teenage boy, who I knew by sight from school approached and offered me two rings. He said he was going to give them to his own girlfriend but they had just split up so would I like them. I naively took them and it later transpired that they were stolen property and he was off loading them on to gullible me. Both occasions resulted in a good beating. Would bad luck dog my adolescence?

At the ripe old age of fourteen, when Dave and I had been together for three months I got myself a Saturday job at our local Mace supermarket.

The country had recently gone decimal. We changed from pounds, shillings and pence to new pence and everyone was adjusting to this strange new concept of having a ten pence piece in place of a two bob coin.

My wages were in this new decimal money. I worked from 4pm till 6pm on Thursday after school, 4pm till 7:30pm on Friday evening and all day Saturday. I was paid the princely sum of 14.5 pence an hour. This worked out to £1.50 per week!

My job was to help customers to pack their bags at the till point. The supermarket also offered a delivery service. The groceries would be boxed, delivery address details written on the side of the box and put out in the stock room until the van driver returned from delivering the last batch. Mum was the van driver at this time.

All this boxing of groceries was my main responsibility. I helped out on the wine and beer kiosk when the store was busy and filled shelves too.

I quite enjoyed the work but would delight in causing mischief in the boxes of groceries if the customers were rude or too demanding. I would shake up fizzy drinks or squish cakes or pats of butter.

Mum and dad still provided my school uniform and school shoes but they said I could now afford to save up and buy all my own clothes!

Most of my wages went into the till at Chelsea Girl. Clothes from there were badly made and didn't wash well or last very long but that was where teenagers did their shopping.

Dave was a talented artist and was commissioned to paint murals in the art block at school. He spent as much time in the art block as he could. This was the year he was taking his GCSE's. He had already taken his

GCSE art a year early and would take A'level art aged sixteen. When all that was done he got a place at the Northampton College of Art.

When he did go away to college my parents and I took him to the YMCA in Northampton where he was boarding because Dave's parents didn't own a car.

I cried all the way home and all week until he came home for the weekend. We spent all weekend together and I cried every time he went back to Northampton on the bus on a Sunday night.

We would write to each other at least three times a week and when my parents had the phone installed it was at least once a week that Dave phoned.

Our relationship had moved on and the shy mnemonic messages became true love letters. I loved him so much I thought my heart would break every time we were apart.

The weeks at school were endless and as I was now studying hard for my GCSE'S it was doubly stressful. I sat mock O'levels and studied hard for the real thing in a years time.

Cheryl and I would work together whilst listening to music. At the weekends I spent all my time with my darling boyfriend.

CHAPTER THREE

The summer of 1973

Dave and I had been together for two years. When he came home for the summer holidays I thought I would see more of him but it was not to be. I was fifteen and he was seventeen. He needed to get a summer job to help finance college fees. Dave got a job with a cleaning company that specialised in industrial cleaning. During factory shutdowns the places would be thoroughly cleaned. It was absolutely filthy work. Dave was often much dirtier than his stoker dad after crawling inside tanks and boilers to clean them.

My parents, Paul, Jayne and I had had camping holidays for the last three years. Dad had bought a large frame tent and all the gear when we first started so it would follow that it was an annual event. I moaned about going and because I was too young to be left at home alone, and would get into all sorts of mischief it was agreed that Dave could come away with us too.

He was told to get a small ridge tent, sleeping bag, pump up bed and so on together. All the camping gear was loaded into a trailer and hitched to my dad's estate car. The six of us went for a weeks' holiday to Tenby in Wales.

The frame tent was large enough for us all to have meals in and at bedtime Dave was separate in his own little tent.

I don't remember much about that holiday but I know it gave us a perfect opportunity to have some intimate times together in that little tent.

Mum, dad and the twins would go off leaving us at the campsite. I wonder if they really thought that people only had sex at night?

We had often been alone at Dave's house. We'd even been alone in my mum's dining room. Mum and dad might have been in the next room but didn't disturb us!

We had had a few occasions where we had done more than was legal already. Most teenagers are sexually active before it is legal, I'm sure. That is what the statistics tell us anyway. I was so in love with him, I wanted to show just how much with my craving, confused teenage body.

The summer holidays wore on and my parents decided we could get away for another weeks' camping. This time we went to Holt in Norfolk. Dave couldn't come because he had to work, he was going back to college in a fortnights' time.

This holiday was nowhere near as good as the previous one when my darling boyfriend had been with me too. It was a disaster holiday. I remember eating prawns, and being violently sick in the night. Was it food poisoning? I came out in a rash all over my face, which diagnosed on our return from Holt as shingles of the face.

When we were packing the car up to come home I walked into the tailgate of dads' estate car and got a black eye!

What a sight I was when I saw Dave, I had a big black shiner and a spotty face. It was a disastrous holiday for the others too. Jayne had grazed her thigh badly on a breakwater (racing Paul along the beach and misjudging the height of the breakwater)

Paul had been bitten by a dog and had to go to hospital for a stitch and a tetanus injection. So all in all we were all glad to be home.

The shingles cleared fairly quickly and the shiner faded but the sickness continued. This couldn't be mere food poisoning now surely? I was going to die!

Most meals ended up in the toilet and I felt nauseous all the time.

I was back at school now and as the days got cooler I dreaded going outside at playtime. My boobs were agonisingly painful when they got cold, so much so that I could have wept with the pain. The sickness continued and the invalid food mum gave me [bread soaked in warm milk] made things worse.

When I was working at the Mace I seemed to be throwing up more often, the smell in the stockroom, a combination of beer, polish and cabbages, always sent me to the toilet at speed.

I was also agonisingly tired and would come home from school, go to bed and wake up the next morning. All these symptoms should have added up but I was very much in denial. I COULDN'T POSSIBLY BE PREGNANT.

We were actually on our way to the doctors when mum said, "your periods are alright aren't they?"

"Yes, fine," I replied.

My stomach sank to my boots, I had missed them for quite a while (how long?)

It couldn't possibly be, Dave had used a condom most of the time. It didn't happen to girls like me, did it?

Eventually I saw our old doctor and he asked, "have you been intimate with a boy?" The truth was of course I had. We hadn't always had full penetrative sex so how could I be pregnant? Surely a baby didn't happen until you wanted one to.

I didn't know how to say any of that so replied meekly "yes".

The doctor went on to examine me and pronounced me approximately five and a half months pregnant. It was official, I could no longer convince myself that it couldn't possibly happen to me. I'd been in denial, now I had to grow up and grow up fast.

From that moment on my life as it was, ended. The world turned upside down, inside out and back to front. My life took a momentous and cataclysmic turn, which would take years to disentangle. Maybe we had conceived the baby in Wales. Were those few moments of pleasure going to be paid for the rest of my life?

The first person to be told the grave news was my father; mum stormed into the house and proclaimed, "YOUR daughter is five and a half months pregnant!"

Anger and tears and heartache would be the only things I would feel for the rest of my life.

I've often wished that I wasn't such a coward; I really should have committed suicide. Many years later I would echo those sentiments and again wish I had been stronger.

The next thing to happen was a meeting of the parents. They had never had cause to meet before. Both sets got together and decided that as I had been to the maternity unit and been confirmed five and a half months pregnant; too late for an abortion that adoption was the only avenue left open.

No one, at any point along the way asked what Dave or I really wanted. All decisions were taken away from us. The year was 1973, not many years previously I would have been sent away to have my baby.

My dad in his fury involved the police and both Dave and I were interviewed. I'll never forget the shame of sitting and telling a young policewoman the intimate details of Dave's and my sexual activities.

She wrote the statement for me and went back over the previous twelve months. She asked constantly, "did we have intercourse, did we use a condom?"

I just made it up as I went along, I couldn't remember back that far, who would? I just wanted the interview to be over.

Dave never told me how bad his interview was but I was told that he might have to go to prison.

I was assigned a social worker and she talked to my parents and me about how things would progress. It's unbelievable, but mum actually started knitting. We were told that we would have to provide several items of clothing and bedding and nappies (towelling ones in those days.)

I was told that when I went into the maternity unit to deliver my baby, if everything was straight forward, I would probably be kept in for ten days and on my discharge I would have a meeting with my social worker there.

I was interviewed at school and told that I could still take my GCSE's in a few weeks time before leaving school forever. School was really hard for me as fellow students were so cruel. I've blocked most of the nastiness that I had to endure but know it was a really difficult time with more tears and stress than ever before.

There would be five girls in that school year group to become' gymslip mums'. My cousin Christine would be the other black sheep in my family, becoming pregnant soon after. Everyone was quick to tell us how stupid we had been but nobody would ever know the price we would ultimately pay.

A trip to Mothercare to buy smocks and all the baby things we needed found me at the checkout. The girl on the till asked me kindly what I was hoping for and I replied that I didn't mind. This simple question for some reason brought everything home to me; this bump was real, I was really going to have a baby.

People saw me as a happy expectant mum but in reality this couldn't have been further from the truth.

Mum was adept with a needle and made a smock and trouser suit in school colours and by the time I sat for my final exams I looked like a beached whale in maroon.

Then I left school for the final time. I would sit out the rest of my pregnancy at home. I would accompany mum shopping or visiting relatives. Dave was at college and continued to write and phone and at weekends we were inseparable.

Christmas of '73 arrived and I remember having a particularly heavy cold and a temperature and didn't feel like visiting relatives. I was forced, miserably, to go because my dad was adamant that Dave could not come and keep me company at home. I was already six months pregnant, how much more serious trouble could I get into?

I would certainly be paying for the shame I had brought on my family for years and years to come.

1974 came in without celebration. I had my sixteenth birthday two weeks after that, the baby was due around the third or fourth week of March.

My pregnancy was a fairly healthy one once the all day sickness stopped and I became heavier.

I craved the large sweet Navel oranges and would eat so many of them; it was obviously very good for me and the baby.

My antenatal appointments were attended with loathing because even though the nurses called me Mrs Crooks, my shame at being an unmarried mother oozed out of me and my own mum was always there with me to add to my embarrassment. I often felt glares of disgust directed at me.

Time ticked on and I tended to stay out of the way a lot of the time during the week; at weekends I'd go round to Dave's house. Hilda was always so kind to me and showed genuine concern for my condition.

Dave was as loving and gentle as ever and although we never talked about it we both regretted deeply that it had happened to us. We had been unlucky but we just had to get on with it.

February ran into March and the end of the month was in sight. I saw Dave at his house on the 30th and complained of a little bit of backache.

I eventually walked home and after a milky drink went straight to bed. Jayne and I shared a bedroom then and both she and I were fast asleep when we were rudely awakened by my gasping as the first stage contractions racked through my body.

I couldn't believe how much pain I was experiencing, to begin with there were large gaps between contractions, when I would doze.

It would have been about eleven o'clock when the first spasm struck. I didn't really connect that the baby was coming for about another six hours. The pain got worse and far more frequent and I had no choice than to wake mum and dad at about 5.30am.

My waters didn't break at home; they were broken for me when I went into the delivery suite.

Mum and dad hurriedly got dressed and made the dash to the maternity unit in no time as there was little traffic at that hour of the morning.

I was examined and told that I was almost ready to go to the delivery room. I was soon going to get the signal to push.

I had nearly left it too late, I'd done most of the hard work on my own. I was shaved and given an enema [which didn't have time to work] before I was taken into the delivery room. I was put on a trolley; legs secured up in stirrups and told to start pushing.

It was an incredibly messy business. I was on my own. I really hoped I was going to die just to end the cruelty.

At 7.30am after ripping open and also being cut, my daughter was born weighing in at six and a half pounds.

Mum and dad had stayed in the corridor for the two hours it had taken me to deliver her. No one even considered that Dave might be able to be with me. Mum came in briefly to see me and then she and dad went home.

Dave was told I'd had a girl and that visiting time was 6–8pm for partners only. Of course, he could have come much sooner than that, they didn't tell him that there was general visiting from 2–4pm.

I must have slept for a little while and when I came round the curtains were drawn around me. I needed the toilet and so put on a dressing gown and went to find one.

When I got there I was amazed at how battered and bruised I was and the amount of ragged stitches I could feel down below.

I didn't feel a sense of things coming to a conclusion. I just felt bereft and lonely and maybe just a bit angry at a woman's lot; even though I wasn't a woman by a long way. How come Dave was pain free?

When I was discovered out of bed I was in trouble. The nurse said that they liked to check that patients were OK to go to the bathroom in case they were faint at all.

I felt fine, just felt chopped up and kicked about between my legs. Maybe this was the continuation of my punishment.

The baby was fast asleep in what looked like a fish tank, she was all pink and perfect, I knew she was mine because her nametag on her wrist and ankle said Baby Crooks, female, 31/03/74.

I think I must have missed breakfast while I was down in the delivery room so when lunch arrived at midday I was famished and more than ready to eat whatever was put in front of me. The other ladies in the bay were friendly enough and the four of us got to know a little bit about each other.

I had to be careful not to give away my situation, it was my worst nightmare.

The lady directly opposite me would have been what the nurses call a geriatric mother. I don't know whether she already had a large brood or had left having this baby quite late. I thought she was totally nutty, the way she kept up a constant conversation with her day old son, as if he would answer her. The other three babies in the bay were girls, so this silly woman had them all down as potential girlfriends for Christopher.

After lunch it was time for an enforced nap before visiting time. This was the worst time for me as I was such a fidget and was totally unused to sleeping during the day.

My baby had been given a bottle by one of the nurses and had had a nappy change.

It was expected that from now on I would be the one responsible for these very fundamental needs.

When visiting time came I was the only one without a visitor straight away until mum and dad arrived an hour later. They stayed a short while, mum doing the proud Nanny bit for everyone in earshot. They checked I didn't need anything and took their leave.

Visiting time finished at four and tea would arrive at five. I was desperate to see Dave. It was so cruel of them to keep him away.

Finally, on the dot of six he arrived, kissed me fondly and admired our beautiful daughter, he even nursed her. He said he would like to call her Lena and I thought it was the most perfect name in the world.

I was so very much in love with him for being so gentle and caring and couldn't drink enough of him in.

All too soon eight o'clock arrived and he had to leave me to go home. I was so tearful I thought my heart would break. That was the first day of Lena's life coming to a close. We would only spend ten short days together Lena and I before she would be taken to her new family. The bonding process was started, we'd already had nine months together, so it didn't take more than a few moments to love her forever.

The pattern of the days was much the same as the first one, nurses checking blood pressure and temperature and stitches, meals arriving and tea trolleys and drug trolleys coming and going.

Whenever I slept someone would wake me up, I was becoming quite ragged. The afternoon naps were utilised more sensibly; no more fidgeting. Lena was no more demanding than the next newborn but it was very hard work.

Bathing, changing, bottle preparation and feeding all took time. There was my own personal hygiene to see to, and salt baths were the order of the day.

About four days into my confinement a nurse came to look at my stitches and told me that they would have to be re-done. I was given something to make me sleepy and wheeled down to a theatre where I was put back in the stirrups and sewn up for the second time.

Dave came to see us every day, Hilda would proudly visit and so would my mum and dear Mam-mam, the proud great-grandmother. I even had an aunty or two come to visit. Looking back on those ten days in hospital I think they were some of the cruellest days of my life. How could anyone with an ounce of compassion put a young girl through such an ordeal? The utter cruelty was unbelievable and I took it all as the punishment I had to endure.

I suppose babies up for adoption nowadays are taken straight away from the biological mother.

Lena was a lovely placid baby who loved to be nursed. This was surprising considering that her presence in my womb was largely ignored and essentially regretted.

Eventually my ten days of confinement were up. The day started like any other until it was confirmed that I would be discharged later that day.

I bathed and got dressed in clothes I hadn't worn for ages. I wasn't carrying any more weight than I had before I was pregnant. I remember putting on a pair of nicely fitting white trousers and a turquoise shirt. The 'nutty' lady in the opposite bed made a comment on how lovely I looked because she was going home that day but in her shapeless maternity wear.

Mum and Dad arrived to take me home and I just had one more job to do.

I had already bathed Lena and dressed her in a white baby grow and hand knitted matinee jacket, bonnet and booties. These I had knitted myself. I had wrapped her in the softest white shawl and taken her in my arms for the last time.

I walked along the corridor and handed Lena over to my social worker, Mrs Witham. She took her from my arms without any words. What words could have been used? She took her from me and walked out of the room and turned right, I walked out of the room and turned left and went back to the ward to collect my bag and say goodbye to the other women.

Only Mrs Nutty was naive enough to ask where my baby was and I mumbled some unbelievable rubbish about forgetting my bag and walked out of the ward. I walked along the same corridor again and outside into the spring sunshine to my dad's car. That was the first day of the rest of my life without Lena. The separation hurt then as much as it still does today.

CHAPTER FOUR

April 1974

We drove home in relative silence and arrived to a quiet house. I think Paul and Jayne were either at school or out with friends. I don't really remember. All I had to remind me that I had just had a baby were the uncomfortable stitches, forcing me to sit on a rubber ring for the next few days.

The following weeks and months were a blur. I was simply going through the motions of my life without being conscious of it.

I was blocking everything out that had happened in the hope that it had all been a bad dream.

Meals happened and the family would gather round the table together. I think even some visiting of other family members went on but I can't really recall anything of note to write about.

Lena was born on the last day of March, April came and went and I think maybe May did too. The cruelty of my ten days in hospital was surpassed only by my parents' actions on my return from hospital.

They never mentioned Lena again; it was as if she was just a figment of my imagination. The old family legacy of not talking about things in case emotions got in the way was very much in evidence.

It was more than I could confront, I knew I had been bad and this was my ongoing punishment. Worst of all, my parents never asked how *I* was feeling. There certainly wasn't any counselling in those days; you just got on with life.

Dave was as loving and caring as ever but he didn't want to talk about his ordeal either. We weren't able to share our grief then and to this day we can't comfortably talk about the situation.

Two months after Lena was taken from me I had an official looking letter. Inside were the typed forms telling me that she had been taken from foster parents' and placed with her adoptive parents. That was the only correspondence I ever received. My social worker had told me that I could never get in touch with Lena. That was the law. Amazingly, twenty-seven years later I was given letters and a photograph that my parents had kept from me.

*

At the beginning of June '74 I had an interview at Marks and Spencer and was lucky enough to secure a place as a sales assistant. I started work there on the 22nd of July 1974.

I can vividly remember my first day. The sights and the sounds and the smells and feeling for the first time in a long time that maybe I would be able to find some purpose in life again. I had to be strong for my own sake or I would probably lose my mind. It was a fantastic opportunity to turn things around and make a career with the company. I know my parents were proud but even those positive emotions weren't expressed.

Two years previously I had broached the subject of staying on at school. My dad's response was "**girls don't have careers, they have babies**". Well, I had proved that theory correct!

So maybe now I could go on to make my parents proud of me. This was to be my grand plan. I had made one mistake, a gargantuan one at that and had taken the punishment metered out. Now I would pull myself up by my bootstraps and get on with things.

I absolutely adored working at Marks and Spencer, it was a great company to work for, very much a family affair.

Nearly everyone I knew, when I joined, had a close family member working there too. Everyone knew everyone and it was only a little store in those days. It went on to have numerous extensions and extra floors added over many years.

Each day held a myriad of experiences; I had a lovely mentor called Ada who really did teach me everything I knew (I sadly attended her funeral in April 2012). I made lots of new friends, some of which remain dear friends to this day, and I enjoyed being grown up in a grown up world.

Bearing in mind this was still 1974 and I was sixteen years old. I was earning the princely sum of £16 with a £2 bonus each week; I thought I was a millionaire.

*

There were often elaborate cocktail parties to celebrate 25 years of service or retirement or leaving and these were tremendous fun.

The lunchtime Christmas parties were fantastic, with the management team dressing up and serving us. The wine would flow and we'd return to the sales floor a little bit giggly. Oh, such happy memories when I didn't believe I'd ever be happy again. I once got so tiddly at one of the Christmas parties I was put in the medical room bed to sleep it off.

My working week was never a chore and my weekends would be spent with my beloved Dave, now in his second year of college.

I still always cried when he returned to the YMCA after the weekend. So he started to travel back on Monday morning instead of Sunday evening so that we could be together for longer.

We were still very much in love and still are. He had spent a lot of time at his brother's house doing up and re-spraying an old Lambretta scooter and would ride back to Northampton even on the coldest of days.

I remember one time when he actually came off the scooter and tumbled head over heels down a steep hill with the bike rolling after him. Luckily he was unscathed but the bike was a bit of a mess. The handlebars were at six o'clock instead of quarter to three and Dave had to ride several miles further to the YMCA with them like that. Once there; they were sorted out fairly quickly. He would often travel back on very cold days with newspapers layered under his clothes for warmth.

There was only ever one blip in our relationship and that happened when Marks and Spencer had building work done to increase the size of the store.

When the extension was near to completion 'bolster staff' came from all over the country to help us get displays ready in the brand new part of the building.

What happened was that a boy called Frank was amongst the workforce. As bolster staff they were all away from home and staying at the Bull Hotel.

The rest of us youngsters would meet up in the bar some evenings and I got to know Frank. What started with a bit of flirting became more serious.

Bearing in mind that Dave and I had been together since I was thirteen years old, I had only really had him as a proper boyfriend. Mainly it was infatuation on my part.

I took Frank home to have a meal and meet my folks. My parents thought he was a much better boyfriend for me. They were trying desperately to break up Dave and me and would have preferred a monkey to him anytime. They always maintained that Dave was too quiet for me. The upshot of it was that I finished with Dave and started going out with Frank.

Mum and dad were thrilled and started treating him like a son-in-law.

When all the building work and preparation for a grand opening was finished and after one more party all the extra staff went back to their own Marks and Spencer stores.

Frank was a native of Basildon in Essex and so after his return there he came and stayed at my house at weekends. From there we would go out in his car somewhere or meet up with my friends at the local pub or disco. Other week-ends I would catch the Kings Cross train and change for Basildon where I would spend the weekend at his house, in the coldest bedroom I have ever experienced.

Frank's mum and dad lived on a main road and the traffic noise was unbearable, I never got used to it and slept very badly.

There was just Frank at home; his elder sister was married with children. I got a very distinct impression that Frank's mum didn't like me. When his mum and dad were out he would always pounce on me and clumsily have sex with me.

I never told Frank about Lena. It was just a guilty secret that had to stay hidden. It had now become my own habit not to talk about it.

Weekends in Basildon, we would meet up with Frank's friends and go to disco's.

Sometimes Frank was the DJ, an avid Beech Boys fan, and I would spend the evening watching him. I turned seventeen in the January of 1975 and around that time it was my turn to go to Basildon. That particular weekend I arrived at the station and as usual Frank was there to pick me up. We started arguing about something and it got quite heated. The row ended with Frank hitting me hard in the face.

I turned straight around and got on the next train home. By the time I got back to Peterborough and had rung home to get my parents to pick me up I had a thick lip and a dark bruise showing above it.

They were horrified because they had held Frank high regard. I on the other hand realised just how stupid I had been yet again, I had thought that the grass would be greener on the other side. My little fling had back fired on me

I wrote telling Dave what a fool I'd been and he took me straight back into his arms. His mum and dad welcomed me back into their hearts too, they had hated seeing their son so upset and lonely when he occasionally came home. We went straight back to where we had been before, Dave coming home every weekend and writing love letters and phoning.

I loved him more than ever and felt even more dirty and used.

Dave celebrated his nineteenth birthday in February of that year and Lena's birthday was fast approaching.

All too soon the 31st of March arrived and Lena was one-year-old.

What was she doing? Who did she love? Who loved her? What colour eyes did she have? What colour hair did she have?

All these questions and a thousand more would spin around in my head at different times of the day and especially at night.

Potentially, I now only had to wait another seventeen years before Lena would surely come and find me. If only I knew then that the wait would be far longer than that I might not have had the strength to carry on. Dave was still resolute about not talking about her and with each passing year he knew to handle me with kid gloves around the time of her birthday. I was simply in mourning. He was still blocking what he'd been through.

Sure enough April would follow March and I would just have to shake myself and get on with life. The spring wore into summer and we were at Dave's house, we decided that we wanted to spend the rest of our lives together.

On the 16th of July 1975 Dave put a white gold solitaire diamond ring on my finger and we were engaged to be married.

We celebrated with a few close friends at our local pub.

This was the final straw for my parents who believed deep down that somehow I would end up with anyone else but David Hudson.

When we had finished they were so happy, they knew that if I was forbidden to see him that I would defy them anyway. Just like Adam and Eve again and that blasted forbidden fruit.

The way that they dealt with not getting their own way over this turn of events was to throw me out onto the street, literally. They had stood by me during my pregnancy and had watched me starting to make a career at Marks and Spencer but this was all too much for them. The morning after our small engagement party I was getting ready to go to work. It was a Saturday. Dad popped his head round my bedroom door and said, "mum and I are going to the club as usual tonight and when we get back we don't want to find you here." I was totally gob smacked, you could have knocked me down with a feather.

I went to work and spoke to my personnel officer about my dilemma. She assured me that it was all said in the heat of the moment and it would all blow over by the time I got home. Little did she know how strongly my parents felt! I couldn't even give her a true account of the history of the matter. The damn skeleton was rattling away in the cupboard but still couldn't be spoken about!

I did my day's work and on finishing at six in the evening I cycled home. I went straight to my bedroom and lay on the bed reading a book. I was trying to be inconspicuous. What would happen when they went out to The Ex-Servicemen's Club? Soon enough I knew. Dad again popped his head round the bedroom door as he had done that morning and said, "we're going now, I meant what I said and when we get home you had better not be here."

So it really was going to happen, I had incurred their wrath for the final time and aged seventeen and a half I would be out on the street.

It was a warm July evening but I picked up my sheepskin coat in case I really was to sleep in a hedge. I put the contents of my underwear drawer into a carrier bag and left the house forever. I had always been brought up to think about clean underwear!

So, armed with a good heavy coat and a bag full of knickers and bras I set off into the world. I hadn't gone far before the enormity of it all hit me; I had nowhere to go!

Dave and his family were in the throws of entertaining German visitors in the shape of Hilda's sister and brother-in-law. This was tantamount to a royal visit and appearances had to be maintained. Dave and I were to be presented as a blissfully happy newly engaged couple the very next day. But tonight, Saturday night, I would supposedly be at home. Even though this was a crisis of considerable proportions I didn't consider bothering Dave or his family but would go round for afternoon coffee and cakes tomorrow at two o clock to maintain appearances.

What on earth was I going to do until then?

My parents had assumed that I would run straight to Dave's house but they were so wrong. They had gone past the stage of caring, that was the problem.

At the top of my road was a pub called The Heron, I only got as far as there and sat down on a bench to think about my predicament. I couldn't even get a drink as who ever heard of a nice girl going into a pub on her own!

It was a balmy evening maybe I could sleep on the bench. That was stupid, I was bound to be moved along at closing time and I needed somewhere less conspicuous. Where could I go? My best friend Cheryl was away on holiday, there was nowhere safe.

The places where we had gone to play as children were down by the clay pits and the brickworks and were not safe places for a girl out on her own. I had always been frightened of the stories of tramps being burned alive in the kilns. Stories went that they had taken shelter and were not noticed and bricked in to die. I'm sure their ghosts would haunt me tonight.

Suddenly my knight in shining armour came along, one of my school friends and fishing buddy of Dave's, Mick Tuttlebee. He asked why I hadn't got anything more exciting to do on a Saturday night than sitting on a bench outside a pub and also why I was clutching a sheepskin coat. It was a wonder I hadn't been accosted sooner really. I explained the dilemma from start to finish; about Dave having to do family stuff and Cheryl being away.

Mick listened carefully and had a little think and said "come on, I'll pitch a tent down by the river for you, you'll be alright there."

This is what happened, unbeknown to anyone else in the world; we went down to the backwaters and pitched a small ridge tent. We installed a foam mattress and a sleeping bag and a small Calor Gas lamp. By now it was twilight and the stars were coming out. I can't remember having anything to eat or drink and Mick kept me company until he couldn't stay out any longer.

Then I was all alone in the tent and outside I could hear rats or water voles scurrying about, I don't think I was ever so low in spirits.

I was conscious that I was rocking and keening and thought that I was losing my mind, maybe I was. I don't remember sleeping but at some point I must have done.

The next morning Mick came back with a primus stove and we breakfasted on tinned tomato soup with fresh milk from the nearby farm. (We knew the farmer's daughter because we went to school with her). That soup tasted so good, I will always remember it. Probably I had come through the worst night of my life and would survive after all. Later that day I went to meet Uncle Herbie and Aunty Marga as arranged, showing off my engagement ring and beaming. We ate cream cakes and drank coffee as if everything was normal and perfect.

It was only as I was leaving to go 'home' that I was able to quickly tell Dave that I had been thrown out, and the details of my new lodgings. I wished everyone a cheery goodbye and said to Dave "see you tomorrow darling." What an actress and what a web of lies!

I unfortunately had to spend a second night in the tent until the German visitors were safely on their way to the ferry and back to Germany.

I don't think they were ever told about Lena or my estrangement from my parents. It wasn't that Hilda had lied especially but was stretching the truth or omitting some of the facts. The real fact of course, was it really was taboo.

The very next day I started living at Dave's house, there was never any question of me finding somewhere of my own.

I waited until I knew my parents were out, went back and cleared all my own things and brought back my bike so I could get to work as normal. I was home. The first few weeks in the Hudson household were a time of adjustment for us all. Mainly it was down to Hilda and her patient nature that melded us together as a family. That patient nature which Dave inherited was our mainstay for the rest of our lives together.

CHAPTER FIVE

July 1975

Dave and I made the most of all the extra time we could spend together; in the early weeks I occupied the small bedroom at the front of the house. After a settling in period, Dave plucked up the courage to ask his mum if we might share the same bed and she didn't seen to mind at all. When all said and done we had had a child together. I remember her bustling in on us the first morning that we slept together and saying cheerily, "Hello you two monkeys, what are you up to?" I almost died of embarrassment and shot under the covers to hide my blushing face.

I was made to feel as if I'd always lived there and I have to admit I was not a bit homesick, nor did I miss my parents although I did miss Paul and Jayne.

I was allowed to cook and found a real interest in what went on in the kitchen even though I wasn't very good at it. Hilda knew this and gently coached me in the science that had eluded my own mother. She very quickly became my surrogate mother and the one I would hold in higher regard as the years went by. My mum would come to the end of her life passionately jealous of Hilda and all that she was to me.

Hilda was a superb all round cook, where as my mum could bake cakes and pastries but lacked imagination when it came to catering for a family. I know my dad was loath to congratulate her on any new meal, as she would serve it for the next four nights in a row!

Sometimes after he had completed a twelve-hour shift she would present him with tinned tomatoes on toast with cheese on top, as she couldn't be bothered to cook anything else. Maybe it was a catch-22 situation where dad didn't praise and so she couldn't be bothered to produce something interesting or exciting.

My parents were newly-weds in 1953; the fifties saw the introduction of 'convenience foods', so consequently if it didn't come out of a packet or a tin we didn't have it. Whilst still at school I opted for school dinners, which were pretty bad then, in preference to Mum's cooking.

One thing she did quite regularly was to mix up Cadbury's Smash, which I hated with a passion. To camouflage it she would fry the whole disgusting mess. The reality was that this took longer than peeling real potatoes.

My brother was a fussy eater and this added to the problem. He was pandered to and had to have something different from the rest of us. We knew without going into the kitchen what was on the menu that night. Fish fingers on Monday; beef burgers on Tuesday; savoury pancakes on Wednesday; stew and dumplings on Thursday and fish and chips on Friday. It didn't alter very much from that schedule.

Mum struggled with her weight and if she was trying to cut down a bit, Ryvitas were constantly on the menu. As a growing youngster you have to eat an awful lot of Ryvitas to feel full.

That summer Dave finished college and was working for the industrial cleaning company. When that contract finished he got a job as a forecourt attendant at a fuel station. He was also actively looking for work as a newly qualified Graphic Designer.

I was at Marks and Spencer during the day and enjoyed coming home to Dave and to do housewifely jobs like washing and ironing.

As Dave only lived around the corner from my parents' house it was inevitable that I would see them at some point. In the two years that I lived at Spencer Avenue I saw my mum twice in the street and she crossed to the other side both times rather than speak to me. Christmas 1975 went by and then my eighteenth birthday with no word from them. I did celebrate it in a small way and had lots of gifts to put in my 'bottom drawer'.

I occasionally saw my brother and sister if they called at Dave's house but they didn't tell mum and dad they had seen me and they also didn't say anything about what was happening in mum and dads' lives. They didn't want to get too heavily involved in the rift; they needed to sit firmly on the fence. They were only fourteen years old and the difficult times of their own teenage battles were already underway.

Mam-mam refused to be affected by the rift and insisted I visit her for my tea on a Wednesday. I would cycle the two miles to Eye from M&S and four miles all the way home to Dave's much later in the evening. Mam-mam and I always had a wonderful relationship and could talk about all sorts of things. She was a very special lady who lived to be 92 years old. Sometimes we would sit in front of her roaring fire and eat ice cream, because that was just what we both fancied.

Mam-mam would always come into Peterborough on a Wednesday (market day) and on a Saturday and would seek me out in Marks and Spencer for a little chat. If she had a friend with her she would also come to show me off, she was always so proud of the fact that I had a good job. We always laughed and said that Peterborough would close down if she stopped coming in on those two days. I heard though Mam-mam that my cousin Christine had had a miscarriage but was now pregnant again by the same black boyfriend. There was even more stigma attached to mixed relationships in those days. Christine went on to keep her baby even though the relationship with the father had broken down. She brought him up by herself and he remains an included member of the family today. My Aunt and Uncle saw things differently to my parents. I believe that a number of family members thought that my parents could and should have dealt with things differently but never passed a comment in case there was an argument or the edge of Mother's savage tongue.

Two years previously, my cousin Jean had been in the maternity unit having her second baby at the same time I'd had Lena. We hadn't seen each other as Jean only stayed one night when she was visiting Peterborough. Katie should have been born in Jean and husband Barry's hometown, Leicester and so was shipped back there as soon as possible. Mam-mam told me about Katie and what a beautiful toddler she had become and my heart constricted tighter for Lena.

Another year drew to a close and I had another Christmas in exile, my second.

Eventually Dave was very fortunate to get a job at Central Printers as a Graphic Designer. Most of the work in those days was done at a drawing board and as Dave was a fine artist and perfectionist this suited him right down to the ground. Nowadays the work is very much computer generated, with not so much technical drawing involved.

The offices were based in the centre of Peterborough but very shortly after Dave's appointment the whole office moved to bigger premises in the village of Eye where Mam-mam lived. We would both go to see Mam-mam whenever we could. We didn't go out much but saved furiously for our future together.

In the fullness of time we decided that we wanted to get married, we had been engaged for eighteen months and it seemed so natural a decision to make.

Hilda said that she wouldn't let her baby go until he turned twenty-one so we looked at a July wedding the following year; in the Queen's Silver Jubilee year. Dave would turn twenty-one in the February. Things moved along very quickly and towards the end of 1976 we started house hunting.

The wedding was set for the 16th July 1977. A reception was booked at the Baker Perkin's sports and social club and Ronnie's brother-in law Ivan who was a DJ was booked to entertain us. Peter, Dave's brother, an avid photographer, would be the official photographer. My sister and Dave's three nieces would be bridesmaids.

With all that done we set about house hunting in earnest. We found a super little bow fronted semi-detached house on the other side of town and fell in love with it on sight. The asking price was £9,400. We had saved up one thousand pounds for a deposit and Hilda helped us out with another thousand pounds so that the mortgage of £7,400 was realistic. Everything went through without too much stress with us being first time buyers and by the end of May 1977 we had the keys to our own home. Dave was twenty-one and I was nineteen. It was all extremely exciting and scary at the same time.

Lena was three years old by now and I had somehow managed to survive her second and third birthdays without losing my mind, maybe there was hope for me yet.

Once we had the keys to Hadley Road we invited my cousins Lynda and Carl and my brother and sister over for decorating parties. The six of us would strip wallpaper or rub down paintwork in readiness for Dave to add his perfectionist touch to the re-decoration. The evenings usually ended in a bit of a party, the six of us really got on well together and some beers or wine were shared. Soon each room was done to Dave's impeccable standard and we could transport a few bits of furniture over.

Dave's uncle Hans gave us a bedroom suite and we bought a brand new bed. Hilda gave us two fireside chairs and that comprised our entire lounge furniture apart from the wonderful stereo system that Dave's parents had bought him for his 21st birthday back in February. We obtained a drop leaf table and six chairs by fair means or foul and that was about the sum total of our furniture.

Our combined record collection was quite large containing plenty of Yes; Emerson Lake and Palmer and the heavier stuff that Dave had got into during college days. My records included some Jimi Hendrix and Led Zeppelin alongside David Cassidy and David Essex. We had been to see the groups Steeleye Span and Barclay James Harvest live in Peterborough so those LP's were in there too.

The people we were buying the house from sold us their cooker and fridge so we were set up. The remainder of our needs came later in the form of wedding presents, like pots and pans and cutlery. We didn't have large items like dishwashers and washing machines on our wedding list like young couples do today. I already had my bottom drawer stuff from my eighteenth birthday.

My wedding dress came from a little boutique in Whittlesey called Louisa's and cost £23.00, my Juliet cap and satin shoes probably cost another ten pounds. Dave's three-piece suit only cost about thirty pounds, so we were pretty frugal.

This was just as well as Hilda and Percy footed the bill for most of the costs of the wedding and between us Dave and I covered the rest.

The wedding invitations went out in May and the number of guests totalled thirty-five people. My parents were invited but declined, although they did allow Paul to attend and Jayne to be a bridesmaid.

I suppose they could have been even crueller and forbidden them to come. My wonderful Mam-mam said that she would be delighted to come; at least I had her. On my side, on the day would only be those three members of my family and six friends beside. The other twenty-four guests would be Dave's family.

So, our big day was fast approaching, Hilda ran up the three small bridesmaids' dresses in powder blue for her three granddaughters' Joanne (six), Julie (four) and Denise (four). She was a wizard on the sewing machine. She also made the chocolate coloured bridesmaid dress for my sister, to complement the cream wedding dress I would be wearing.

I had a hen night out with a lot of my M&S chums at the White Hart in town and a lot of Pernod and lemonade was drunk by me resulting in a cracking hangover the next day. It was one of the most memorable nights of my life and good practice for being centre of attention, which I normally hated. I was as nervous as a kitten about the big day. I remember, even as a very young girl, the thought of getting married terrified me.

It was just as well that both Dave and I had our nights out a whole week before the wedding as his stag night, with a couple of mates, drinking fairy liquids (crème de menthe and vodka) had him swaying home as well! What a cute drunk he made, I loved him so much it really was physically painful. The day was drawing ever closer.

Because I was going to my wedding from Dave's house it was agreed that Dave would spend the night before the wedding at his brothers Peter's house in Whittlesey.

Hilda and I sat up quite late on the eve of the wedding getting the flowers ready. We didn't have any experience in floristry but decided it was the cheaper alternative. We arranged three little baskets of flowers for the young bridesmaids and then concocted a bouquet for my sister to hold. This was the practice bouquet to ensure that mine was as good as it could be. We just got stuck in and wound tape around stems of roses and greenery and wired the whole thing together. When finally finished, the flowers looked as professional as bought ones; my bouquet was a delicate shade of peach.

We laid the flowers in the cool outhouse and went to bed hoping they would be still good in the morning. I was so nervous and excited it's a wonder that I slept at all.

CHAPTER SIX

Saturday 16th July 1977

After such a late night with the floral creations I actually slept remarkably well and woke superbly refreshed. The wedding was to be at midday and so I had a whole morning of careful preparation. I took a long leisurely bath and even managed a little scrambled egg for breakfast (Hilda, forever the mother hen feeding and nurturing everyone). I then went along to the hairdresser's where my shoulder length hair was teased into curls and ringlets and my Juliet cap fitted securely in place.

I then returned home and spent lots of time carefully applying my make up. Next came the big moment when I could put on my dress. Suddenly, the butterflies arrived in my stomach and I realized that this was all real and by lunchtime that day Dave and I would be man and wife. My something borrowed and blue was a garter lent by one of Dave's work colleagues who had recently got married. My something old was a pair of earrings. So I was all set. The neighbour who was going to drive me to the register office came to say it was time to go. Mr. Rusdale was the father of a school friend of both Dave and myself and lived opposite us in Spencer Avenue. I remember saying as I got into the car, "Oh, Mr. Rusdale,

I feel sick" and I did feel absolute dreadful, not because I wasn't one hundred per cent sure about Dave and myself but was feeling phobic about the bride role. Looking back I don't suppose I was any more nervous than any other bride.

We drove to the register office and then drove around a bit to be fashionably late. Eventually I had to get out of the car and make my way to the foyer where Dave was smilingly waiting. We joined hands and made our way into the room where we were going to be married, followed by all our guests. The sun shone brilliantly and everyone was happy, no one more so than me. We took our vows, I remember faltering on one of mine and had to have it repeated to me, as I stood like a goldfish with my mouth wide open! It was nothing more than a nervous brain fade.

Dave said all his vows without a single mistake and beamed throughout the entire ceremony. Percy and Dave's uncle Hans were our witnesses. Soon enough the ceremony came to an end or at least the speaking part did and the time came for Dave to kiss me. He kissed me and held me with such tenderness that told me he would always look after me, it was heavenly.

We were then ushered along to sit down at an imposing desk to sign the register. Dave managed that without any problem, as did our witnesses but 'clumsy fingers' Helen managed to get ink from the fountain pen all over her hands.

It was just a tiny bit of bad luck, which sent the Registrar and the Assistant Registrar into a spin to protect my beautiful cream wedding dress from ruin. This they managed with handkerchiefs and tissues gleaned from somewhere in the room. It caused quite a commotion and I'm sure it meant that the next wedding was running late!

Out into the brilliant hot July sunshine, it was an absolute scorcher of a day. Confetti and rice were thrown abundantly and some great wedding photos taken. I recall that in the fantastic heat the rice in my hair swelled and left a starchy mess! It didn't take too long with so few guests, so the little bridesmaids didn't have time to get bored.

I was starting to relax a little only to discover that my wonderful new husband was suffering from a heavy head cold and was sniffling and snuffling. His nose was getting redder and redder from the continual nose blowing. Poor darling, I'd just promised I'd look after him in sickness and in health, looked like I was starting off straight away.

On to the wedding reception at Baker Perkins' Sports and Social club where a finger buffet was laid out on the prettiest tables I had ever seen. Little fresh rosebuds had been pinned all along the edges of the tablecloths and little posies were dotted around each table. All the blooms were the same gorgeous peach that I had in my bouquet.

As Hilda now worked for Baker Perkins she had hired the complex relatively cheaply and the Chef she worked with had provided the finger buffet for an amazing 35 pence per head.

Our wedding cake was made by my mum and dads' next door neighbour, Joan. She was someone else whom Mum had fallen out with, they hadn't spoken for years. Joan had a soft spot for me and had offered enthusiastically to make my cake. The discussing and then collecting of it had been cloak and dagger stuff because each time I visited I ran the risk of being seen by Mum or Dad next door. Nonetheless for that, it was a wonderful gesture and a wonderful wedding cake.

When we first arrived at the reception Dave spotted Ivan, the DJ in the large room beyond the foyer and strolled off to have a chat with him. And that was where he was when all our wedding guests arrived!

I was so embarrassed to be standing there on my own, not being able to get Dave's attention to get him back to receive our guests. A few minutes passed before I was able to ask a waitress holding a tray of sherry to go and fetch my new husband. I hadn't managed to hold on to him very tightly so far, I would have to address this pretty rapidly!

I discovered that all the rice that had landed in my hair had congealed into a starchy mess in the heat of the sun. Someone has since told me that they believe that little hitches are good luck. We certainly needed some good luck in our lives.

Dave's mum had put one hundred pounds behind the bar so that everyone could have a drink with us. It was yet another lovely idea of hers that made the day go so fantastically.

The reception was hugely enjoyable and I can honestly say I loved every minute of it. I chatted and circulated and soon it was time to get started on the buffet. The top table seated the bride and groom, witnesses and their partners. The small number of other guests could spread themselves out. It was an enormous spread for so few people and everyone started to tuck in. We discovered that the quiches had an unusual sweetness to them, which wasn't unpleasant. (The Chef had requested one of his minions to whisk eggs and milk together and they had assumed the mixture was for egg custards and so put sugar in!)

As it was such a stiflingly hot day the large double doors to the playing fields had been thrown wide open and the little ones played out in the fresh air. It was some time later when someone noticed that the children were returning to the buffet table for plates and plates of food. When we went to investigate, half of the kids living in Dogsthorpe were down at the bottom of the field having a picnic, word had got around and more children were arriving by the minute.

My parents sent a telegram! What a disgraceful thing to do, considering they had boycotted the occasion they should have left it at that. I lived to regret even acknowledging the wretched piece of paper that was their only effort towards my wedding. As time went on they would be the ones living to regret their actions.

All too soon it was time to take our leave, we were not going away on honeymoon but were going straight to our very own little house.

It was decided on the spur of the moment that everyone would go back to Hilda and Percy's to see our wedding presents, so that was what happened.

I took the opportunity to change into a long gypsy skirt and cotton blouse, it wasn't a 'going away outfit' as we weren't going away but it was more comfortable than my wedding dress. We had started to make a move to go 'home' to our own home. We realized that Mam-mam had no easy way to get back to Eye. Dave and I said we'd do a round trip to see her home safely first. This entailed me sitting in the back of our Reliant Robin while Mam-mam sat in the front, she was in her seventies, we couldn't expect her to get in the back! So there we were, with the bride out of sight in the back of the van with 'just married' scrawled all over it and a very elderly lady in the front with the Groom! Tins and old boots rattling along behind. Not the most romantic of starts I'll have to admit.

I will always say, it's not what you make of your wedding day but how you live and love during the rest of your married life together that count. This was the first day of the rest of our lives. I knew we would get that bit right. Forever and ever but just three years too late for Lena to be part of our lives.

*

We had the little Reliant Robin because up until May of that year, when Dave passed his car test, he held a motorbike licence. The three-wheeler car was a dry form of transport and he was legally allowed to drive it on a motorbike license. I had never been a very confident pillion passenger on the back of Dave's Lambretta and that was why we got the Reliant. I do believe nowadays that the 'plastic pig' is billed as a classic car!

The summer before we got married we had set off on a trip to Holkham beach with a picnic. In those days seat belt wearing was not compulsory but on this occasion because we were going on a long journey we did both 'clunk-click'. We had only gone a few miles out of Peterborough, we were on the Thorney straight, as it was called when Dave flicked his cigarette out of the quarter light window, lost concentration and one of the rear wheels clipped the kerb and flipped the car over. The car somersaulted several times and we travelled 369 ft. and 6 inches on our roof before coming to a stop upside down on the opposite grass verge.* On stopping, the windscreen simply popped out and lay in one piece on the grass verge too. During the smash my door had been wrenched off and part of the skid along the road had taken the skin off my thigh. I had also been twisted and twisted into my seatbelt and couldn't get out. There was a strong smell of petrol and I was frantically trying to get out. Dave got free and raced round to my side of the car and was able to release me. I was gently laid on the grass verge, I overheard one of the rescuers saying to another, "I thought we were going to bring them out dead!"

The ambulance came very quickly and we were taken to Peterborough District Hospital where all our cuts and bruises were declared superficial and we were discharged. We actually went home from there on the bus! Bearing in mind that Dave's dad didn't own a car, we had no one to call to collect us from the hospital. So, I had escaped from my second car smash.

---

*The police officer who came to see us the next day gave us this data. He cautioned Dave for driving without due care and attention.

CHAPTER SEVEN

Saturday 16th July 1977

Back to our wedding day and after taking Mam-mam home to Eye.

On our return to our own little house I realized that I was absolutely famished, I'd eaten very little at the wedding reception because I'd been so excited and also because I was busy circulating and gossiping with family and friends.

It was no good, we both decided that we were hungry so Dave went out to get a Chinese takeaway. I don't ever remember a Chinese takeaway tasting so good. Soon after we'd eaten and cleared away I looked out onto our patio to see our neighbour motioning us outside to chat over the garden fence. This was very friendly of her, but it was our wedding night after all!

It took us ages to get away from Anne. In the eleven years that we lived in that house I don't think we ever had such a long conversation with her again.

We were finally on our own and could get on with some loving. We spent the whole night enjoying each other and finding out how tenderly we loved and how much we were in love. It was like a fairy tale, we were totally immersed in each other. It didn't matter that we weren't on some tropical island or in a romantic city, we only needed each other. Dave was and is my soulmate forever. The two weeks we had off from work for our honeymoon were spent doing things together and doing things in the house. It was a getting to know each other time, a lovely tranquil time.

On my return to work, after the honeymoon, I thought I'd better ring my parents to say thank you for the wedding telegram. I did this at the earliest possible opportunity, Monday lunchtime. We didn't have a phone at home so I used the booth in the staff quarters during my lunch hour. I rang because even though I had been incommunicado for two years I didn't want to be accused of bad manners as well.

I fully expected my thanks to be icily acknowledged and then to carry on as before. I realized many years later that this would have been a better outcome. Mum answered the phone and after listening to my thanks promptly burst into tears. Full of remorse like the time with the skipping rope. I think they had both realized that they had lost that particular battle, it was a done deal and I had married Dave, there was nothing they could do about it.

Looking back they were like a couple of children who had taken their ball in because they couldn't get their own way. There was nothing else to be gained by sulking so they had decided to play ball again. After all the angst of the last two years I wished I'd been stronger and not gone straight back into the family fold.

It was agreed that I would go and visit them the very next evening. On arriving home from work for the first time as a married woman I was just happy to cook for my man. I still wasn't a very good cook but I was trying really hard to please Dave. He had said on more than one occasion that the meal I had produced "wasn't like mum's cooking". Hilda was a very hard act to follow, I was starting to lose some of my confidence. We all have to start somewhere in order to get years of experience in the kitchen, my time would come!

The next day I pulled out all the stops and made a minced beef pie, all from scratch; no convenience food today. The only trouble was I didn't realize that you had to fry the mince first. I just gently cooked the whole listeria packed pie and served it with new potatoes and vegetables and gravy. When Dave came home from work I lovingly presented it to him. He pushed it around the plate a bit and then told me it didn't taste quite right. I think at this point I lost my temper and said that that was all I'd heard for the last fortnight about Hilda's wonderful cooking and my mediocre efforts. This was probably our first row and I would learn later that night that Dave was right and I was wrong. After clearing away the dinner pots and washing up it was time to go over to see my parents for the 'making up' get together.

Dave said that he would drop me off there and wait for me at his mum's house, spending precious time with her. This he did, dropping me off and driving round the corner to Spencer Avenue. Thinking back, I imagine that Hilda was feeling quite hurt. After all she'd done for me, taking me in and making sure I was safe. That I would go back to my parents at the first click of their fingers. All the wedding plans and the outlay had been dealt with by Hilda and here I was just two weeks down the line back in my parents clutches, the Crooks' were back on the scene as if nothing had happened. That old cliché about blood being thicker than water! Well, I rang the doorbell and Ranger barked fiercely, as usual and I was let in, he didn't seem to mind that two years had passed and was delighted to see me. Equally so with Mum and Dad, they made a fuss of me and as usual they didn't talk about anything meaningful, that way it wouldn't become an issue or an argument. We didn't do the post mortem on the rift in case another argument flared up out of it. They made small talk and the only reference to my married state was when Mum asked to look at my brand new wedding band and matching engagement ring. They, of course, hadn't seen the engagement ring before either. They asked why I hadn't brought Dave round because now that we were married he was accepted too! How hypocritical was it possible to be? The upshot of it was they were back in control. I walked round to Dave's mums' and brought Dave back to my parents' house for him to be in-lawed. When we got back, Dad shook Dave's hand and Mum kissed him on the cheek and those gestures alone were the only indication that they had any regrets. They just didn't ever say that very important word, sorry. At the end of the day they stayed away from our wedding because they didn't want us to marry, what message were they giving now?

If Dave were not such an easygoing character he would have felt quite put out by their behaviour. He very magnanimously followed my lead and as long as I was happy he was happy. We were back in the bosom of my family!

The evening wore on and we were becoming more comfortable in their company, we even shared a beer. Dave disappeared to the toilet and was gone for ages. Eventually I found him sitting on the back door step a most peculiar shade of green. He said that he hadn't been able to move away from the toilet as he had been violently sick and then had suffered severe diarrhoea, he was sweating profusely. Oh my goodness! I had given him food poisoning. The only thing for it was to whisk him home, to our own home where he would be more comfortable. As it turned out, because he had been so violently sick, he had got the poison out of his system and so recovered very quickly. We didn't eat minced beef for a long time after that!

We parted company with my parents, leaving them with an invitation to come to our house as soon as Dave was feeling better. It was all as if nothing had ever happened. It was just like the day I came home from the maternity unit, tired and emotional; nothing was spoken about.

Whatever was wrong with healthy discussion, it was as if they were worried about becoming confrontational and clashing swords with us? I think they lost out by not doing a post mortem on the whole sorry mess but they preferred their silent way. Only a few years would pass before Jayne was in a similar situation, but that is another story to be told later.

In July 1977 the Queen celebrated her Silver Jubilee and we had gone over to Mum and Dad's to watch their newly acquired colour television, considering we had only been back on talking terms for such a short time, it was a fantastic occasion.

When we got home around nine o'clock in the evening we found a street party in full swing in our street to celebrate the Jubilee. Because we had only moved in two weeks earlier we hadn't been involved in the organization of the event but soon got on with enjoying the party and meeting other neighbours in the street.

What a night that was, there was dancing and singing and lots of drinking!

Only three weeks after I was married I achieved my second ambition, to drive.

I took my test on the fourth of August 1977 and was fortunate enough to pass first time. The funny thing was that on the big day they called out "Miss Crooks", I explained that I was now Mrs. Hudson. The grumpy old examiner said, "just sign as Helen Crooks so we can get on with it." I thought to myself, there's no chance of me passing this driving test today, but carried on regardless.

Was it legal I wondered, had I committed a fraudulent act? We set off after reading a car number plate to make sure I could see well enough. When I attempted my three-point turn I did it in about ten and stalled as many times! The beads of perspiration stood out on my forehead. When we were finally facing in the other direction he asked me to pull over. I thought, "that's it, I've blown it, he's going to drive us back to the test centre."

He calmly said, "pull yourself together and when you're ready, we'll continue". Off we went again through the town (it was lunchtime) and we got stuck at a zebra crossing for at least five minutes while shoppers trailed across the road in a steady stream.

On our return to the test centre he asked me a few questions on the *Highway Code* and then proceeded to give me a pass slip. Wow ! I was absolutely astonished and asked him if he was sure, he replied that he could give me the other type if I really wanted.

I scuttled out of that car quicker than you could say 'pass' and back to my driving instructor who congratulated me warmly, confident that I would pass anyway. Oh yes!

It was hours before Dave was due home so I tackled my housework with a silly grin on my face and plotted to pretend that I had failed. When Dave got home from work I did just that and put on a long sad face when he asked me how I'd got on. He commiserated and said, "never mind darling, you can put in straight away for another test". He then realized that I had been joking and was amazed that I had passed first time. Dave had passed first time only three months beforehand. It called for a celebratory drink down at our local.

Mum and dad soon fell into a pattern of visiting regularly and the four of us went out on most Saturday nights together. We would go to the Ex-Serviceman's Club where Dave and Dad would play billiards and Mum and I would chat in the lounge. Later in the evening a game of bingo would be the highlight. Some Saturdays we would all go out to a country pub and we would go back to our house for a supper of cheese and biscuits and coffee. We somehow just settled into this comfortable closeness.

My parents were impressed with what Dave and I had managed to achieve, in good jobs and our own home, but they never said as much. They bought us a coffee table to help add to the amount of furniture in our spartan lounge, this was their late, and only contribution to our wedding. They'd managed to marry one daughter off very cheaply, the cost of one coffee table!

*

During my two years of exile, Dad's health had deteriorated and he had suffered kidney failure. After being diagnosed with renal failure he had started to go to the Leicester General Hospital three times a week for dialysis treatment. There wasn't a renal unit in Peterborough in those days. Sometimes he would drive there by himself, endure the six hours of dialysis and then drive the forty miles home; other times mum would accompany him. All this had happened without my knowledge, how could I have known when there was only silence?

I think mum was bitter that I hadn't been in touch earlier. She didn't like it that I was as stubborn as they were. In reality I wasn't being obstinate but just getting on with my lot as best as I could, it had been them who had thrown me out. How was I supposed to know about things that were happening if no one was communicating with me?

Nowadays, Dad only had to go to Leicester for weekly check-ups because he did his dialysis at home. Their dining room had been converted to a mini ward with a huge kidney machine dominating. Dad would sit or lie in a recliner chair with large needles with tubes attached to this monster of a machine for eight hours at a time. He continued to work his shifts as normal (he still worked as a printer) and if it meant dialysing during the night that was what he did. It did mean that during that time in his life he would be either working, sleeping or on the machine.

He managed to juggle it all rather well with mums' help. After using the machine it would have to be stripped down and sterilized and rebuilt with brand new membranes (the things that do the job of cleansing the blood).

Mum and Dad usually did this job together but if I was around I would help him instead. Paul and Jayne had finished school and were looking for jobs, they were both at home. If I had a day off in the week, usually a Thursday, I would go over to mum and dads' and sit with dad while mum went shopping or did something else. Jayne and I would take turns in keeping Dad company and also making sure that the machine was running smoothly.

We were both the same, in as much as, we could only sit in his room for a limited period before needing get out.

We would sit for a time and then make an excuse to leave the room, maybe to make a cup of tea. We would then sit with our heads between our legs, breathing deeply until the faintness passed! We would then get prepared to go back in with him and repeat the whole process again. Jayne would come out and I would go back in and vice-versa. I don't think he ever found out that we were dreadfully squeamish.

The fact of the matter was that there was an awful amount of blood going round in those tubes. It was also a big responsibility, if the machine ever failed we had to help to take him off, it was all very frightening. We just had to hope and pray that a matching kidney would soon be found.

It was sometime shortly after Dave and I were married that the old dog, Ranger had to be put to sleep. Some weeks previously he had chased a cat down the garden and caught his dew claw in the fence ripping it clean out. This had eventually caused him to limp badly and at the very end he'd dragged his front paw, he was a sorry state.

We all took his loss badly but Dad took it worst of all, he refused to ever have another dog. My sister and I said many years later that our parents would have been better off sticking with dogs as relationships with humans were always difficult.

CHAPTER EIGHT

Christmas 1978

On our first Christmas together as a married couple, Dave and I hosted a family gathering. There was Mum and Dad, Paul and Jayne, Uncle Maurice, Aunt Iris and Cousin Peter and Mam-mam. I only had a little galley kitchen but somehow produced prawn cocktails, roast turkey and all the trimmings followed by Christmas pudding and cheese and biscuits for the ten of us. The meal was a success and probably marked the start of my love of entertaining at home. The afternoon of card games and chatter ran into teatime. Out came a buffet tea of sandwiches, cold meats and pickles, sausage rolls, trifle, Christmas cake and mince pies. I really don't know where we put it all in those days but it was a family tradition. I suppose it did soak up the copious quantities of alcohol we consumed !

Not finished yet! Round about nine o'clock the whole buffet would come out again and also with the cold meats would be bubble and squeak.

Paul and I would man the frying pans, giggling drunkenly. I don't think it would be a good idea to add up the number of calories we consumed in that one day.

I think it would be nearer to a weeks or a month's worth of calories for some less privileged souls.

Bearing in mind, it was only one day out of a four day holiday. We would go to Mum and Dad's on Boxing Day and to Uncle Maurice's the next day and do it all exactly the same, all over and all over again.

I know that some years later when we did the healthier options it would be Mum and her brother Maurice who would bemoan the loss of the frying pan at suppertime or even the lack of suppertime. My word they could put some food away!

Some of that gorging harked back to the time of the depression when there had been very little food on the table and Mam-mam had been a young bride. When I was a young girl at Mam-mam's house over the Christmas period the spread had been much the same, with as many as twenty-five people round the table.

But this wasn't 1926 it was 1977 and a time of plenty all year round. Although, earlier that year there had been some shortages, I had queued for bread several times since I'd been married and we had had power cuts due to the miners' strikes.

*

New Years' celebrations were always big events in the family so it was quite normal for Dave and myself to stay over at mum and dad's house to see the New Year in. We would play cards all evening and toast the year in with Big Ben on the television and then carry on with the party.

Only when we were too intoxicated to stand would we set about inflating our pump up bed and fall about laughing helplessly until it was finally achieved. A good lie in and hangover cures and quiet were the order of the New Years' Day.

My birthday was soon upon me again and I would reach the grand old age of twenty, Dave turned twenty-two in February and Lena would be four at the end of March. What was she doing, what did she look like, was her hair long or short? Did she have lots of little friends? Did she go to nursery?

The weeks and the months just kept rolling round.

*

February of '78, Mum and Dad celebrated their silver wedding anniversary. The whole family went out to dinner to help them celebrate it. Sometimes we could be just like an ordinary family. It was a lovely achievement for them both as Dad's health had been in the balance. A picture appeared in the local paper of the smiling couple, with the by-line about Dad's home dialysis.

*

Dave and I camped in Cornwall that summer of '78 and we were now the proud owners of a Sunbeam Rapier in metallic orange. It was a fantastic car to drive and I took up driving again because I never had felt confident in the Robin after the accident.

In order to sell the Reliant Dave had had a new fibreglass body put on the chassis of the wreck and had used it for a while. The poor ill-fated thing needed some welding doing to it so Dave had already dropped the price.

The new owner took it to a garage to be welded where upon the wretched thing caught fire and melted into a blackened mess on the garage floor! The garage owner gave the guy another car from the forecourt in place of the poor old 'plastic pig'. He got a good deal out of it after all.

We had travelled down to Ladram Bay that July in brilliant sunshine and pitched our two man tent. It started to rain and it rained for the whole week! What a disaster, we had to try to cook on a single ring primus stove and it rained and it rained and it rained. We should have given in gracefully and come home, but we didn't. We thought our love would keep us dry!

Dave took me to a very classy restaurant to celebrate our first wedding anniversary where we spent more on the meal than we'd ever spent in our lives. If my memory serves me right, the bill came to about £35; back then that was more than a weeks' wages. The only really dry place was the car so we did a lot of driving round Cornwall but not getting out to see very much because of the persistent rain. Evenings were spent in the clubhouse and when the week was up we were glad to be going home.

The summer before we were married we'd spent a fantastic fortnight in Looe in Cornwall in adjoining flats with Peter and Jenny, the weather had been wonderful. We had to pretend to be married and I wore a cheap ring (from Woolworths) for effect. I think in those early days we thought we'd like to retire down there. A decade later Peter and Jenny did migrate to Devon to live.

Dad was getting on well physically with his home dialysis and was still on the waiting list for a kidney transplant. Mentally the strain of his illness was having an effect on their relationship and I was called over one day to referee a fight. Mum was quite a good nurse and Dad was a long suffering patient but this particular time the sparks had flown!

It all boiled down to the fact that they were under each others' feet for long hours while Dad was on the machine. I think they both felt frustrated and trapped. I also think they were taking each other for granted, not appreciating each other's strength in the care and support they were giving one another.

Anyway, I had rung home from work and Mum was in floods of tears saying that Dad was going to switch off the dialysis machine (always the child) and she didn't know what to do to make him see reason.

I went to my manager and explained that there was a crisis at home, he phoned for a taxi for me and sent me off to sort things out telling me not to return until I was happy to do so. That was the sort of caring company M & S was in those days.

I was able to calm the situation and get them talking to each other which they always found difficult, and went back to work in the knowledge that Dad wasn't going to do anything foolish.

*

I was constantly trying to be the perfect daughter and would spend the next three decades bending over backwards to do just that.

I would invite them over for Sunday lunch regularly, sometimes Mam-mam would come too. Mothering Sunday and Fathers Day were always grand affairs. When they had milestone birthdays I put on surprise parties and contacted long lost friends.

I was always telling them that I loved them but I never felt I was doing enough to make up for that one mistake. I would, and still do beat myself up over it. I was wearing sackcloth and ashes all of that time too.

*

The next really sobering event to take place was that my dear Uncle Maurice died, he was still a young man in his mid forties and left behind his wife Iris and my cousin Peter who was only nine years old.

Maurice had complained of stomach pains and had eventually gone to see the doctor. He was admitted to hospital where they discovered that he had a cancer in his stomach, which was inoperable. They simply closed him up and cared for him as best they could, he only lived six short weeks after that.

We all knew that he was dying but Mam-mam (his own mother) wasn't told the whole truth and she took it really badly when he died. He was her youngest child. No one knows the utter feeling of loss until you lose a child, you just don't ever expect to outlive your children.

I was particularly fond of Uncle Maurice and took his death badly. I went to see him in the chapel of rest (this was the first time I'd ever seen a dead body) and I had nightmares for a little while after. On one occasion I had woken and looked over to see Dave sleeping and as I looked he metamorphosed into Maurice, I was absolutely petrified!

The day of the funeral was traumatic, and not having lost anyone so close, since my Gran, when I was ten, it was really tough for me.

Aunt Iris was trying to do the best by everyone but ended the day with an argument with my mum. This resulted in them never ever speaking again. I think my mum had said something along the lines that Iris had never made Maurice happy and had made his life a misery. What a cruel and nasty thing to say to a woman burying her husband. Mum was never able to put herself into someone else's shoes.

So, just another feud to add to the list, my mum never imagined it was anything she had done wrong. She truly believed that she was right and everyone else was in the wrong.

I continued to see Aunt Iris and Peter and even went on to have them over at my house for the following Christmas holiday on Christmas Day. This went down like a lead balloon with my parents; they stated angrily that they wouldn't be in the same house as Iris and Peter so they stayed at home. Yet another instance of Mother throwing all her toys out of the cot! I took great delight in the fact that when I said Iris and Peter would be spending Christmas with us, they did just that. I was starting to loosen the controlling hold they had over me. Mum and Dad didn't want it to happen but I was able to stand by my decision and carried it through. It was my home and it was my life. I was never going to allow them to dictate to me again.

I had thought they would join us and heal the rift, but realistically I should have known better. Once they had set their minds on something it was impossible to shift them.

Mam-mam was so upset by Maurice's death that she never really got over it. She said on more than one occasion that she wished that it had been her instead of Maurice that had died.

I tried to coax her back to the living family that loved her but she was inconsolable. She also spent that Christmas Day 1978 with us, to the absolute disgust of my parents. Let them stew in their own juice, the childish pair. With Christmas over we looked forward to the New Year and we did spend that with my parents and brother and sister.

That year (1979) I was twenty-one and the twins were eighteen so Mum and Dad decided to throw a joint party for the three of us. The whole family was invited, at least those that were on speaking terms, and dozens of friends for each of us. The final figure for guests totalled about 150 people. Mam-mam, Mum, Jayne and I would do the catering and the venue was The Leeds Hall in Eye. My birthday is the 15th January and Paul and Jayne's the 13th of February so we choose a date roughly in the middle of those two dates. Round about the first Saturday in February was booked. The disco and the outside bar were also booked. The invites had gone out with Christmas cards so we knew that 150 people were expected.

On the eve of my 21st birthday (15th January) I just knew that my darling husband hadn't got me a present or a card and as it was a Sunday evening, he was in a mess!

What he was thinking about was the party early next month and had literally overlooked my actual 21st.

Well, I gave him hell, this was supposed to be a really big milestone and he hadn't marked it. The very next day he went out and bought me a silver gate bracelet and a beautiful card but I was my mothers' daughter and threw it back at him and said it was too little too late. It would be a long time before I really forgave him and I obviously haven't forgotten to this day!

A week before the party it had snowed and to start with that was fun. Unfortunately the City Council were striking for more pay and the roads weren't being gritted. With each new layer of snow it became more treacherous. After a week of freezing conditions the roads were rutted ice rinks and not a pleasure to drive on at all.

We had to carry on regardless and on the actual day of the party Dad ferried us to and from the hall to set up tables and to start the catering. Mam-mam was our resident expert as she had 'done' more wedding receptions than hot dinners. On some of those occasions I had helped her and had even been known to serve behind the bars after helping with sandwich making.

On arrival in hazardous conditions we saw that the High Street was completely clogged with lorries parked up nose to bumper. The weather was worsening and the lorry drivers thought it wise to stop while they were safe. Someone had seen movement to and from the hall. As Mam-mam lived close by we had ferried food from her house to the hall on foot as it was marginally safer.

The lorry drivers came to see if they could get a cup of tea and somewhere warm for a while.

We ended up putting tea and coffee on for fifty-seven lorry drivers, this put us behind in our preparations. Afterwards we realized we should have charged them for their drinks and sold them as much food as they could eat. Only half of our guests got to the party later that night because of the terrible weather. We were left with a mountain of food.

The party started at seven and only a handful of us were there, later a steady trickle of guests arrived to swell our number but not the one hundred and fifty who were expected, maybe eighty all tolled.

Needless to say we had a great time, there was plenty of food, the disco was great and the wine flowed. One unfortunate event was that a few village yobbos' gatecrashed and almost spoiled it.

All the grown up men formed a posse and threw them out on their ear. Dave was the only one to stand up and say a few words to congratulate me on my 21st and the twins on their 18th and to ask mum up on stage to receive a bouquet of flowers to say thank you for the party. I said a few nervous words of thanks too.

I loved him so much for doing that, let's be honest no one likes public speaking, but protocol meant someone had to say something. At the very end of the evening we had a lot of clearing up to do and at long last we could venture out into the night and hopefully home safely.

It had frozen solid again and we had to walk back to Mam-mam's to see her home safely and to get our car.

Dave fell over on the ice and split his trousers from waistband to waistband; I told him off because it was his wedding suit and it was only its second outing. I would now have a big sewing job on my hands. Mind you we laughed and laughed,

We had already been married for two years and life was good, we were very happy. We had a fairly good social life and were considering other holidays, maybe not the camping kind! We even had a surrogate child; a gorgeous female marmalade cat called Tammy. We had her a few months and she went off and got herself pregnant.

She wasn't exiled? Oh no! She was pampered and loved. When her kittens were born she chose to have them under our bed so we had to move them.

She was a very good mother and cried bitterly when all but one of the kittens were sent to new homes. We kept one female tabby, a grey, black and white one and called her Susie. Mother and daughter got along as best they could for the rest of their lives together, mainly spitting and swearing at each other. A little bit like my relationship with my own mother!

Dave and I never spoke about having any more babies. I personally didn't want any yet as I was still grieving for Lena and I think Dave as always just kept quiet to avoid any stresses and strains, anything for a quiet life!

*

Later that year Mum celebrated her 60th birthday and I put on a big surprise party at my house. I invited all the family and some friends and neighbours. I bought her 60 red roses (in December they are quite expensive) 60 mini chocolate bars. Silly things like that always gave me pleasure.

I even asked one of my young male work colleagues to get done up in a 'dicky bow' and be the waiter for the night.

There just had to be any excuse for a celebration.

Later that year dad decided to retire and I put on another party for the whole family. It was an excuse to get together but ended up being a bit of a sham because dad went back to work for a further eight months. Then he retired officially after that.

CHAPTER NINE

The 2nd April 1982 one of dad's wishes came true. He received a phone call at work to go to Leicester General Hospital as soon as possible; they had a kidney that was a good match for him. After five years of dialysis this was the most welcome news he would ever hear. Dad soon packed a bag and was on his way; I don't know how he drove himself there under those conditions, but he did.

Mum stayed at home and paced the floor; I think in her place I would have gone with him and stayed with him. I think she chose to stay at home because she lacked the confidence to drive home on her own. She would have gone if one of us had been able to go with her but we were all working. So we waited for news that he'd had his operation and then for updates on his condition when he came round.

The next day, after work, mum came to pick me up from work as soon as I finished and we drove to Leicester to see Dad. Paul and Jayne came too, so there were four drivers in the car for the return journey back to Peterborough. I think Paul drove back on that occasion because by the time we were half way home it was getting dark.

Mum especially hated driving in the dark, maybe this stemmed from the accident in 1957, I don't really know for sure.

When we all got into the ward to visit dad he looked a million dollars, he seemed to be positively beaming with good health. You could see he was absolutely thrilled to see us all and was like a puppy with two tails. After so long suffering with poor health he had made up his mind that a positive approach would lead to a speedy recovery.

And this is what happened; he spent the required time (about three weeks) in hospital and did everything the nurses told him. Mum went to visit every day but always managed to cajole one of us accompany her. As I said before, it was for the long journey home later at night.

Soon the time came for him to come home, it must have been a fantastic feeling for him, it was a fantastic feeling for me and I hadn't even done anything. We celebrated with gusto; dad was even able to enjoy a small amount of alcohol after such a long time of abstinence.

When people are so kind as to donate their organs, they and their families can't begin to imagine the joy they bring the person who receives their kidney or pancreas or eyes or heart. This also extends to include the families of the people given an extra go at life, it feels very special.

Dad was really fantastic, it wasn't a pain free ride and he had to endure a lot and he did it without complaint. He needed to consume copious quantities of tablets and in the long term they would have a fatal impact on his health.

But his new kidney was young, his new lease of life was young and everything was rosy in the garden. He went back to work and was thrilled to be leading an almost normal life again.

We thought it would last forever but in fact that kidney lasted ten years before rejecting.

Soon enough life settled down to some semblance of order and everyone got along fine for a while. This is what life is all about; you spend most of your life bumbling along until you hit the next brick wall.

The next crisis to occur in the Crooks' household was the following year. My sister Jayne met a guy who was recently separated from his wife. Jayne didn't cause the split, it had already reached stalemate and the children involved were older teenagers.

This relationship may have fizzled out fairly quickly but my parents did the same to Jayne as they did to me and threw her out.

They basically said that if she couldn't live to their very high moral standards while she was under their roof then out she would have to go. Yet another case of my parents falling out with someone when they couldn't get their own way. She did go and she set up home with this guy Malc and spent some time with him. They shared a mobile home near to where Dave and I lived and we saw them often.

We even went on holiday to Ibiza for a week with Jayne and Malc and two of their friends in the summer of '85.

It was a total disaster as the friends, whom we didn't know, the husband was an alcoholic. He spent the entire holiday either throwing up or falling down. The villa was right on the end of the runway and the reverse thrust noise was almost unbearable as the planes tried to stop.

The worst thing though was Scottie's abysmal behaviour. Some evenings we five had to creep out when he had passed out so that we could enjoy ourselves. If we allowed him to come with us he would go on a bigger 'bender'.

One day Jayne was driving back to the villa and Scottie was being a total drunken idiot, standing up through the sunroof and shouting insults to passers by. Jayne swung the car into our yard and hit the brakes hard where upon Scottie shot out of the sunroof and slid down the bonnet of the car. We laughed so long and so much that we nearly wet ourselves.

Then to cap it all I went down with a bad stomach and thought that I would have to be brought home in an air ambulance as I was so poorly. I couldn't be more than two minutes from a toilet for many days. Mornings and evenings in the villa, everyone would take their turn in the bathroom but allow me to dive in between each of them. That holiday was my first experience abroad and I remember it for all the wrong reasons.

I was already quite under weight when I went out to Ibiza because I was suffering from anorexia, I continued to suffer right through the eighties. The years of torturing myself over Lena and the controlling way my parents had dealt with the situation eventually took their toll. On my wedding day I weighed in at a healthy nine and a half stones, on my return from Ibiza I weighed a mere seven stone.

I had worked my way up to supervisor level at M&S and managed the food department with a turnover of many hundreds of thousands of pounds and sixty members of staff as my responsibility.

In the seven years of working for the company staff had come and gone and sadly the Personnel Manager Mrs. Cook who was there when I first joined had moved on to another store.

Her replacement was a woman called Sue Somerley who took an instant dislike to me, decided she wanted rid of me and 'got the skids under' me.

She decided that everything I did was wrong where previously it was right. She undermined my authority and generally made my life miserable. I believe that as an anorexic person I only had the control of my weight left in my life, everything else seemed to be going wrong again.

Mrs. Sumerley, at one time, even offered me a job over at our outside warehouse knowing that in six months' time everyone there would be made redundant.

Dave was getting tired of me coming home every evening and crying my eyes out. Not only was I anorexic but I discovered that as I weighed so little it didn't take much alcohol to forget all my troubles and about my miserable time at work.

I was drinking quite heavily and most evenings, collapsing into bed, out for the count.

In desperation Dave went in to the store to see the Deputy Manager about the way she was victimising me. Things did calm down for a little while but the magic and sparkle had gone out of my career.

I would eventually achieve 28 years there and the bitch Somerley moved onto pastures new. I can only hope that she ended up as a bag lady rummaging in bins for left over MacDonald's meals. It's all I can think she deserved. With hindsight I should have left the company a whole decade sooner.

Jayne was still in exile, she and I were, and still are very close so I saw a lot of her. She often said that she had no intention of making up with mum and dad; she didn't miss them in her life at all.

*

Paul, by this time, had met a lovely girl called Karen and was engaged to be married. The six of us, Paul, Karen, Jayne, Malc, Dave and myself got together and had barbecues at Sandringham or Hunstanton and generally got on well together.

As Paul and Karen's wedding got nearer we all realised that mum, dad and Jayne would have to meet for the first time in four years! Jayne said that she didn't have a problem with that and would stay away from them as much as possible. This wasn't a realistic option because of course they would have to stand together for the photographs at the very least. Karen very rightly took the matter into her own hands and stated that if they didn't 'bury the hatchet' then none of them would be welcome to her big day. They decided to do just that and got together before the wedding and made up their differences.

It was a beautiful day. It was everything that my own wedding wasn't. Karen had the white dress and the lovely church wedding. Paul had proud parents there for him on his big day.

I was into poetry writing at this time and wrote most of my family gushy, cheesy poems. Paul and Karen were no exception. I wrote a very lengthy one for their wedding.

The best man came over to me as soon as it was discovered in the wedding card, he said that he had no idea how to read poetry so would I please do the honours. Oh blimey, that wasn't how it was supposed to go, never mind I would have to stand up and read the blooming thing. Better to have it read emotionally by me than badly by him! I was really nervous in front of so many people and when I finished there wasn't a dry eye in the place!

When Wedding Bells Ring

Oh happy, happy wedding day,
What a lovely couple, we all say,
The Ploughwright's join the Crooks' all,
To congratulate our Karen and Paul,
A big new family, young and old,
All together, none out in the cold.

So down the aisle to say "I do" they went,
Let's hope every second is happily spent,
We all sang hymns with gusto too,
And cried happy tears, only a few,
It seems like a fairy tale, but all of it's true,
Eyes lock and they say, "I love you".

Paul in love with his beautiful bride,
So proud to have a wife at his side,
In misty white and so demure,
They will be happy, we can be sure,
You've pledged your love, and now vowed,
To love forever, till in your shroud.

Courting done and getting to know,
The happiness will ever flow,
The setting up home to be together,
We wish them health, wealth and happiness forever,
The perfect start to married bliss,
The single days, you will not miss.

We hope however many years you are wed,
No more tears than that will you shed,
And so dearest brother, these few words,
Are composed from the heart, and have you heard?
How very fond of a new sister I am,
Pray to God for a long lifespan,
So together, you will always be,
In trust; in love; in harmony.

CHAPTER TEN

Life at work wasn't any easier and during that time I was very depressed. The anorexia had become a way of life and I held my weight at only eight stone. I ate only enough to keep alive. Some nights when I went to bed I actually thought I would die in my sleep because I was so hungry. In December of 1984 I wrote this:-

Depression

Everything's wrong and nothing goes right,
I look in the mirror, a terrible fright,
Eyes always watery, threatening to spill,
Tears never far away, no goodwill,
It's all too much, I feel so depressed,
Never relaxing, always stressed,
I don't know why I feel so alone,
Maybe it's not me, could be a clone,
Smiling is difficult, mouth always turned down,
It's easier and comfy wearing a frown,
Mostly I'm happy but now I am sad,
Nothing that happens makes me feel glad,
Maybe tomorrow, or the day after that,
My hormones will unscramble, I'll feel like a chat,
I realise how silly and futile it is,
To get in a panic, a state and a tizz,
So hurry up girl, and get sorted out,
Enjoy life, be happy and forget what it's about.

Dave by this time was freelancing in the evenings for a design and marketing agency in Corby. He was still working during the day at Central Printers and then at home in the evenings on the 'Blaze' designs. He travelled to Corby to pick up or drop off designs every few days. He had been doing this for about three months when he realised that he would have to make a choice between the two companies; he was working so hard keeping two jobs going.

He made the decision to go to Corby daily and gave in his notice at Central Printers. He would end up doing that fifty-four mile round trip for the next twenty years! Nonetheless, he was so very lucky to be doing a job that he was passionate about.

Evenings Alone

Evenings spent all alone,
While Dave works on his own,
In his study papers strewn,
Endless hours, he is a loon.

The restful shades of cream and wine,
And as he draws line after line,
The time just goes, apart we are,
And not an argument thus far,
Drifting apart like cheese and chalk,
Because we never stop to talk,
I know it always pays its way,
Maybe we'll be rich one day.

But in the meantime, what's to do?
A really good chat is overdue,
And smoke and smoke, I never stop,
And drink too much, go over the top,
Then like an alky, I stagger to bed,
My clothes I very quickly shed.

Another day over and done,
It wasn't really so much fun,
And in the morning, another headache,
Dream the whole day away, I flake,
And home again to another drink,
This can't go on, I'll see a shrink.

But David turns a real blind eye,
And over the weeks I really try,
To be a good girl and eat some more,
But drink seems to be the only cure,
Is this to be my slimming fate?
Will my liver disintegrate?

The calories counted are all liquid,
And soon I know I'll flip my lid,
So look out Rawsby, here I come,
Try to cheer up and not be glum.

That poem was written in on the nineteenth of March and on Lena's birthday at the end of March I would be at my lowest ever when I phoned The Samaritans. The woman I spoke to was very sympathetic and listened and even went on to invite me in to the office to chat.

I didn't go in the end but it seemed to be a turning point of sorts.

Jayne was the only one in the family that ever mentioned Lena and would usually ring me on the day and simply ask "how are you feeling?" It was almost like checking that I'd made it past another birthday unscathed.

Lena was eleven and would be going to senior school in September. Was she still alive? Had she run out in the road aged five and been killed by a car? Did she know she was adopted? Did she hate me? I didn't know the answers to these questions.

When Jayne found out that I'd needed to ring The Samaritans she was horrified that we weren't able to talk more deeply. We made a pact that we would always be there for each other and we always have been ever since.

Talking honestly and compassionately had never been part of our upbringing but we found small ways at first to 'council' each other, as that felt more comfortable we talked even more deeply. We had a common bond in as much as we both had experienced exile years. Jayne would say, even to this day, that she regretted reconciling the differences with our parents. I on the other hand spent the whole of the rest of my life trying to make it perfect between myself and my parents, all to no avail.

*

In February of 1985, Peter and Jenny moved down to Devon, they had bought a guesthouse in a lovely part of Torquay. By the June of that year they were ready for business. They decided to have a trial run with guests and invited Dave and myself and three other couples from Peterborough to spend a week with them. What a fantastic week that was, the ten of us never stopped laughing and had liquid lunches and boozy dinners every night. This usually culminated in some of us singing on the stairs outside a particular couples' bedroom door. In the whole week of this happening we never did get that song word perfect! We were a great team and helped Jenny set the dining room for breakfast or for evening meals. I could have really seen myself doing something similar, it was very enjoyable.

Ten Go Adventuring Down Devon Way

A week at Beau Vista is fantastic fun, so sad to leave when it's all done,
Peter and Jenny were smashing hosts, and showed us sights with lots of boasts,
Dave drank jugs of Jolly Old Roger, but in the morning was a model lodger,
Louise wants to know who the hairy one is, if the fire alarm goes don't get in a tizz,
"As I was walking down the street one day" was the song each night they'd try to say.

The 'posers' were showing at Cockington Forge; Graham and Dave had no shirts on!
All week long it was riotous fun; continuous binging, poor old tum,
The kitty worked, everything was fair; we all agreed and Dave said "yer,"
Travelling through villages, three cars in a row, Rona and Arthur in the Morgan made a show
Biggles went through town, amid cries, shoppers couldn't believe their eyes.

Clotted cream teas were such a treat, especially for
'little Steve', his palette is sweet,
Fiona and I lay tables, just the job; things went
smoothly with such a big mob,
Each job took half the time, friendships grew, and we
got on fine,
Dartmoor saw a rare breed of goat; Arthur with hands
in the pocket of his coat,
Anyone spotted a clapper bridge here? We went round
twice in a very low gear.

When 'Big Steve' wore his rugby strip, Fred kept us
talking, in his grip,
"Get it down yer neck" the cry would be, as we had
food or drinks or tea,
And as the week came sadly to a close, a trophy was
awarded for the best pose,
Points were won and lost, all agree? Graham won the
po unanimously,
We'll all be back again next year, look out Beau Vista
and have nothing to fear.

*

The summer of '86 we took Hilda over to Germany for
a visit to her sister and brother-in-law. Percy stayed with
his own sister while we were away. He was already in his
eightieth year and had been diagnosed with the start of
dementia and was on medication for this. I think Hilda
was actually pleased for the respite and knew that he
would be fairly well looked after at Alice's.

It was my first visit to Germany and I absolutely loved it, the scenery was breathtaking. We stayed with Hilda's sister Marga and brother-in-law Herbie at their huge farmhouse close to the Dutch border. Their lifestyle was beyond my wildest dreams. Dave and I cycled around the local area and did all the touristy bits and I was able to pick up a bit of the language.

We even managed to go out with Dave's cousin Karina to a nightclub, where we danced until late. On that occasion a stunningly beautiful German girl with an hourglass figure and blonde hair down to her waist danced over and claimed Dave as her own. She just shimmied in between Dave and myself and made it very plain that she fancied his pants off!

I simply turned to Karina and carried on dancing, I wasn't the slightest bit jealous, in fact I was proud. I knew that even if he danced all night with her, it was me he would be going home to bed with.

Hilda didn't like the way we were treating her sisters' place like a hotel and tried to keep us back at base a bit more. We on the other hand were on holiday and wanted to be busy all the time. She did need us to take her to visit family and friends in the area and further afield but it was the endless cups of coffee and cream cakes that nearly drove us mad. Dave spoke a little German and I spoke none so sitting while the elders chatted was excruciatingly boring.

We travelled up to the Hertz Mountains to mothers' birthplace and spent time doing the same thing in that area. The scenery around there was fantastically spectacular and actually reduced me to tears. An old school friend of Hilda's took us to a border point (the Berlin Wall was still firmly in place then). I have never before or since been to such an eerie place and seen such poignant things as I saw there.

My goodness can those Germans eat? It was just one long round of eating and as I was still struggling with the anorexia and it was a major issue, to say the least. I couldn't insult anyone by refusing food so I managed small portions but this was never enough for Hilda. She had her own eating problems during the war, that of absolute and utter hunger, she couldn't understand why I didn't eat.

This caused a lot of friction between us and ultimately between Dave and myself. I heard her say to Dave one day, "what is wrong with her, she can't eat but she can bloody well drink?"

He of course, had split loyalties; he tried not to upset his mum and he tried not to upset his wife. He ended up not being able to balance the two of us and we really fell out. I told Dave that I'd never go back to Germany with his mum as she played us off, one against the other. I was frightened it would split us up. I can honestly say this was the one and only time that Hilda and I clashed swords, she was always my rock.

CHAPTER ELEVEN

The later part of 1988 Dave and I decided it would be a good idea to move house. Dave had beautifully decorated the whole house twice over at Walton and it no longer held a challenge, we'd lived there eleven years.

Dave's boss at the time had planted the seed of an idea with us because; in his words we were 'grossly under mortgaged'.

As we were both working and on fairly good salaries it was a good investment to go up the property ladder. We started to house hunt; we were looking for an older property that Dave would be able to 'get his teeth into'. In the January of 1989 we put our house on the market. For anyone who's ever moved house they don't need me to tell them just how stressful the process is. I hated people traipsing round my home; it no longer felt like home.

In the late eighties gazumping was rife and we were gazumped three times. Each time this happened and we lost a property I was heartbroken. I always believed that the particular house was perfect for us.

With hindsight, some months later I realised that somehow fate played a big hand and we would never have been right in the houses that we lost.

We went on the market in the January and eventually moved in the middle of November, it was eleven months of hell.

I had done a large amount of packing during July, we had a buyer and things were going ahead with our purchase.

Suddenly our vendors inexplicably withdrew their house from sale and left us stranded again. We ended up walking round the boxes I had packed for another four months!

I remember Dave buying me flowers for our wedding anniversary (July 16th) and he had the presence of mind to buy a vase to go with them as the others we owned were all packed. We often heard the saying "they're packed!"

Even on the day of moving a phone call from the solicitor informed us that the funds had been transferred incorrectly and we would probably have to wait. I informed the solicitor that all our worldly goods were going to go into the removal van and if we spent the night in the van too then so be it.

I left my old property absolutely pristine the new people would be able to simply move in and put their feet up!

When we arrived at our new property it was quite a different story. The people we were buying from hadn't even washed their breakfast pots, which were in the sink. They also hadn't packed up any of their numerous kitchen cupboards. Their poor cat lay in a carrying basket meowing pitifully, obviously fed up with the whole charade.

Our removal men started to bring in the large items for upstairs like beds and wardrobes and the boxes that were clearly marked for the upper half of the house.

I started by washing up the breakfast pots and emptying some of my boxes into the kitchen cupboards.

As a box was emptied I filled it with items outgoing and helped the Davis's with their packing!

It was some time later when we finally saw the back of the old occupants. We worked like Trojans, between the two of us and by bedtime that night, every ornament was in place and every picture was on the wall.

Hilda was fantastic; she told us that our evening meal was at a certain time. We downed tools, went over to Stanground, ate our dinner then went straight back to the unpacking. It was such a help, as without her we would have just kept going until we were ready to drop.

Tammy and Suzie, our beloved cats, spent a couple of days in the master bedroom with a litter tray and didn't like their new surroundings one little bit. They were desperate to be outside.

After two days we let them explore the rest of the house and eventually they went into our lovely garden. They seemed to love the new house as much as we did and settled quickly.

We had lived at the old house in Walton for eleven years but now we were closer to the town.

I could cycle to M&S in half the time it used to take me. My first day back at work I managed to get myself lost on the way home and had to make a serious detour!

It was around this time that I was diagnosed with an under active thyroid. When we moved house I thought it was because the house was big and draughty, I could never seem to get warm.

I would wear a ski all-in-one around the house and sit with my back on the radiator. We had an open fire in the lounge, which I would light and sit right on top of. I went to bed tired and woke up equally tired; I was like a battery that wasn't being charged. I said to Dave one day, "I feel so ill I wish I could die in my sleep."

He said, "You shouldn't be telling me that you should be telling the doctor!"

I went to see the doctor the next day and he looked at my eyes and my fingernails and said, "I think you have an under active thyroid, we'll do blood tests but in the meantime take these tablets I'm prescribing." He was so sure of his diagnosis that he had prescribed thyroxine tablets. After three days of being on the medication I felt a hundred times better. When I went back to the doctor it was all confirmed and my levels adjusted.

*

Not long after we moved, work was still a nightmare and I had a particularly bad morning. It all came to a head and I marched into Sue Somerleys' office and told her I couldn't stand it any longer. I said that I wanted to stand down as a supervisor and become a sales assistant again. Twelve years, I had worked for the company and I really ought to have left. What I said was, "If I am such a rubbish supervisor then I'll be the best damn sales assistant you've ever had."

She took that on board and the following week I was scheduled to move to Menswear.

As I left her office, relieved at my decision, I stupidly stepped off the top of the stairs and fell the full length of the flight, top to bottom. I landed in a very undignified heap at the bottom. Two warehouse men heard the commotion and thundered down the concrete stairs and proceeded to grab one arm each. I shouted, "Don't move me!" because I didn't know the extent of my injuries. As it turned out I had badly gashed my shin, peeling back a large triangular section showing bone. I was taken to accident and emergency where a few stitches soon repaired the physical injuries. The mental scars would take longer to heal; it was as if Sumerley had pushed me off that top step herself. I went into shock as I thought about what might have happened, I could have been wheelchair bound for the rest of my life.

The bitch came to visit me at home and brought a pot plant to add insult to injury. I didn't make her very welcome and she didn't stay very long. The pot plant went in the loo!

After three weeks off, I returned to work. I felt a lot more settled and certainly less stressed. I would carry on in the company for another sixteen years. I was really good at what I did, and to me, that was all-important.

Lena was the same age now as I had been when I had her. Every one of those fifteen years had been tinged with a deep down sadness that was never really going to lift.

It was around this time that Dad started to get ill again, the kidney was starting to reject. He had had that kidney for seven years and he had had an extra seven years of good quality life.

The only problem was, we all thought it would last forever. As the weeks and months went on it became clear that he wasn't getting any better. His check-ups at Leicester brought no good news and eventually the doctors decided to remove the kidney and put him back on dialysis. This meant another lengthy operation and another period of convalescing. Seven years had passed and the home dialysis unit had been removed so it meant three trips to Leicester again to dialyse there.

As luck would have it another kidney became available some months later and dad went on to have yet another operation. We hoped and prayed that this kidney would last longer than six years

We still went out with my parents a lot in a foursome and we did a lot of entertaining at our house so as to get everyone together as much as possible (all my family). Dave's side of the family did get some of our time but not much. It seemed that the Crooks' still held the monopoly on our time.

We took mum and dad abroad with us to Dave's company villa. It was mum and dad's first time abroad and they were like a couple of kids in a sweet shop. The villa is in a very unspoiled part, on the Costa Blanca with fabulous views overlooking vineyards and the sea. Most evenings we saw big firework displays down in the valley.

We all had a fantastic time and they cherished those memories and often looked at the photographs many years later.

Dad was particularly fond of a place we took them to up in the mountains to a place called Guadalest. Mum was struggling there because there were countless steps, she said she would sit under a tree and wait for us to come back. We three, Dad, Dave and I climbed up but when I saw the views I simply had to go back down and fetch her. She still tried to stay under that tree, she was suffering with the heat (being a large lady) and the years of smoking had taken it's toll. I eventually persuaded her to take it one step at a time and we reached the summit and were thrilled with our achievement.

*

Every Christmas since 1985 I'd entertained my parents at my house because Hilda and Percy always went down to Devon to Peter and Jenny's. There was never any conflict about them having a turn at our house.

We tended not to mix the Crooks' and the Hudson's, it never felt quite right, they didn't have a lot in common. I always felt my mum merely tolerated Hilda and was also a bit jealous of the good relationship I shared with her.

Peter and Jenny had some shocking but wonderful news in the autumn of '89; they were expecting their first child after nearly twenty years of marriage. Jenny was forty-two and had a coil fitted but this baby was determined to come into their lives. They started to make plans to sell their guest house and eventually moved to a beautiful bungalow in the charming village of Stoke Gabriel near Totnes.

In the mean time Gemma was born on the 9th March 1990 and they would still be at 'Beau Vista' for Gemma's first Christmas.

Gemma was born some ten weeks early, weighing in at two pounds and seven ounces. Jenny nearly died from pre-eclampsia, all her vital organs were failing.

Poor Peter was in pieces with worry and the whole family prayed that Gemma and Jenny would pull through. She had several weeks in the special baby care unit at Torquay Hospital. She eventually came home when she weighed about five pounds. What a little scrap of humanity she was, but what a huge part of all our hearts she stole. She was special because of the thread she'd hung on to for survival.

Dave and I were invited down to Devon for Gemma's first Christmas along with Nanny Hilda and Granddad Percy.

That seemed a long way off so we took a week off work in September and motored down to Devon to see Peter, Jenny and Gemma. We both fell helplessly in love with the baby and realised that there was something missing in our lives. After fourteen years of marriage it was time to start a family of our own.

While we were away on holiday we talked it through and decided that I would make an appointment to see the doctor to have my coil removed as soon as we got home. We could then start trying to conceive.

It didn't quite work out like that; when I went to the doctor he pronounced my coil 'lost'. I had to wait to be referred to the gynaecology clinic to have an ultra sound scan to find the 'lost' coil. The consultant there was able to locate the coil and remove it quite easily; she told me to go away and get pregnant, she didn't want to see me until then!

We set about making a baby of our own and we were lucky to conceive within five months. I feel so sorry for couples who try and try and are disappointed month after month.

We went down to Devon for Christmas and to cuddle that wonderful little Gemma; who at nine months old was even more captivating than the last time we had seen her.

We saw the New Year in with more expectation than other years in the hope that we would become parents.

We only had four disappointing months when my period arrived and I personally felt it was never going to happen. I thought that we were being punished further for having Lena when we weren't supposed to.

March of 1991 I was confirmed pregnant. It was totally different to seventeen years earlier when I had

Lena. I wasn't as sick and I bloomed with health, the anorexia was a distant memory; I loved being pregnant. No one was going to take this baby from me!

Gracious, Lena was seventeen, only one more year and she would be an adult and would be allowed to come to find me. Would I be a grandmother before I would get a chance to be a proper mother? It was possible.

When we went to tell my parents the good news Dave spoke first. He said in quite an old fashioned way, "We're going to hear the patter of tiny feet!"

My mum replied, "Oh good, you're having a new kitten?" We laughed and laughed.

The scans those few short years ago were quite primitive in comparison to today's wonderful images but all the same really exciting to see.

I continued to glow as the year progressed, I felt so different in every way. I so enjoyed the baby somersaulting and wriggling and couldn't wait for it to be with us.

When I was six months pregnant we helped Dave's mum and dad move from their family home to a two-bedroom bungalow with warden control. It suited them so well and was much easier to keep than the three bedroomed house they had moved from.

The baby was due around the 19th November so I worked until the end of October then started my maternity leave. Up until the end of September I was still cycling to work, a heavy seven months' pregnant.

The last month at home before the baby was due I organised as much as I could towards Christmas, writing and sending out cards, buying all the presents and generally getting ready.

Three weeks before the baby was due I was still waddling round to our local shops but eventually as the head engaged it was too uncomfortable to walk any distance. Mum and dad would pick me up when they went to Sainsbury's for their weekly shopping.

When my labour started at six o'clock in the morning and I knew that it was for real, I just couldn't wait for things to progress along and for the baby to be here. I was so scared but knew that the only thing was to get on with it.

CHAPTER TWELVE

On the 19th November 1991 at 2.30pm, Emily Jayne Hudson, weighing in at 7 lb. 12 oz. came into the world. The midwife had given me the date and she was right on the button. At least this time Dave was with me. When planning for the birth I'd asked him if he wanted to be there and he'd said of course he would be there for me.

This time when the contractions started I knew what was happening; I'd been having Braxton Hicks (practice contractions) for about three weeks. I stayed at home and had a bath then did some ironing in the very early stages, later as things speeded up Dave and I went so Sainsbury's to do some shopping!

There were several contractions during that shopping trip but I just hung on to the trolley until they subsided.

After we got back from the shopping trip I rang my mum to tell her that we were going to the maternity unit; I also rang my sister to tell her that she would be an aunty before much longer. I told them all that Dave would keep them posted. This was before the era of mobile phones being widely used, we certainly didn't possess one.

When I finally got into the maternity unit a nurse gave me a guided tour of the facilities. When a big contraction came over me and I had to stand and hang on to something she informed me I wasn't breathing properly and proceeded to give me a demonstration and a quick training session.

When she eventually realised I ought to be examined me she found me to be nine centimetres dilated and ready to go into the delivery suite.

Dave by this time had parked the car and was with me. Off we went to this beautifully decorated little suite. This was a far cry from the operating theatre I remembered from the last time. Things were going along OK and I was getting nicely high on the gas and air, the midwife had broken my waters with an instrument of some kind.

There I was worrying about making a mess in this plush little room. I was the one fussing about having enough paper down to catch the torrent of water that came from me.

Right at the very end when I was pushing savagely and making a lot of noise about it the monitors were telling the midwives that the baby was in distress. All of a sudden I was plonked in a wheelchair and rushed round to a delivery theatre with more equipment than you could ever imagine.

There were doctors and nurses swarming everywhere. They quickly got her head and then shoulders out and all the pushing was over. Emily was briskly taken and hooked up to all sorts of machines and checked over. I am convinced that had it been any longer she would have suffered brain damage. They didn't say that of course.

I was glad we had all that technology at our disposal and that we weren't at home.

She was given back to us then and we became parents properly.

That very welcome first cup of tea was served, the lights were dimmed and the three of us were left alone.

At the time it felt even scarier than that first time having Lena. Emily was a perfect baby girl and she was ours to keep.

Mum and Dad and Paul and Jayne came to visit with the camcorder, the happy event was recorded for prosperity.

The microphone was clipped to my nightdress and every little sound was recorded, this was only four hours after Emily was born. We only stayed in the maternity unit for four days, once breastfeeding was established, we were sent home. That was scary too.

I was exhausted when we got home and was pleased to be in my own bed that night. I had fed Emily and changed her nappy and settled her in her carry cot inside the cot in the nursery.

When she cried two hours later and I went in to her she was ice cold. It was November of course and the heating was on a timer and would come on again at six in the morning. I quickly brought her into our bed to feed her and to warm her up. I was so scared, what would have happened if she had died that first night?

She didn't die and we both settled into our new roles as parents.

Emily's first Christmas five weeks later was the only one I ever had off. We were invited over to my brothers for the day. My sister-in-law was six months pregnant with their third child but entertained us all wonderfully (Mum, Dad, Dave, Emily and myself, plus the four of them). Emily was surrounded with presents but slept through the proceedings. I was coping alright with breastfeeding but I wasn't a natural. I don't think I was relaxed enough about it. I tried to be super mum and had to have everything just so in the house.

When Emily was just six weeks old we had her christened at our local church. We chose to have it done so early because my family owned an heirloom of a beautiful hand made christening gown belonging firstly to my great-grandfather. It was nearly a hundred years old and had been made for a tiny baby from the previous century. Babies were 'churched' much earlier in those days in the hope that bringing them into the fold early they stood a better chance of survival.

I did the catering myself and entertained about twenty-five people at our house.

I had already joined the toddler group at the local church and met lots of mums to have coffee with. It was my meeting place for new friends for me and for Emily.

In the early days of motherhood I did get half-hearted offers of help from my mum but knew how much she hated doing her own housework so I always said I didn't need anything doing.

When mum and dad came to visit they would always have a cuppa, which I made, and when they got up to leave, the dirty cups would stay where they left them. So I knew the fact that they could just get up and leave a mess meant that the offer of help was half-hearted. They wouldn't dream of taking them to the sink, much less washing them up! So that pretty much summed up the amount of help I was getting. Dave's mum would have done so much more but had no means to get to us under her own steam.

When my mum and dad were visiting myself and Emily, three times a week, they never considered that Hilda might want to come over too. There was that old jealousy rearing its ugly head again.

As the weeks wore on we were getting more used to the constant needs of a baby. Emily was putting on weight but very slowly.

At the baby clinic when Emily was nearly five months old the health visitor suggested I put her on formula milk because she was so hungry. I was very upset to be giving up feeding her myself; I felt I had failed in some way again.

The good thing about bottle-feeding was that Dave could get involved, he loved giving her a bedtime bottle and settling her in her cot. Earlier in the evening she would have a bath with one of us, which was always lovely family time. Once settled in her cot she would gurgle happily until she fell asleep.

As she got older the gurgles would be songs. We once put a tape recorder under the cot so we could listen to her singing.

When she was six months old I went back to M&S but instead of doing full time as I had before my maternity leave I went back to working Thursday late night (5-8 pm) and all day Saturday each week. Mum and dad would babysit Emily for about an hour on Thursday evenings, from the time I left home at about 4.30pm till Dave got home at 5.30. I was cycling to and from M&S in most weathers.

*

I hadn't been back at work for many weeks when I got home one Thursday to find Dave in a right mess, Emily sat in the high chair looking very poorly. She had been violently sick in her cot and had vomited several times since. He didn't know which way to turn and what area to clear up first.

I took one look at her and phoned the doctor immediately. When three quarters of an hour later he hadn't arrived I phoned again. When he finally arrived he told us he had been 'boning up' on the current thinking on gastroenteritis. I was beside myself by then and he called me a neurotic mother.

The diagnosis was gastroenteritis and he prescribed some sachets of fruit flavoured medicine to rehydrate her. She soon made a speedy recovery and life returned to normal again.

When cutting teeth she seemed to suffer with nappy rash and I would battle against it on a weekly basis. What I discovered after some time was that if Emily had a dirty nappy whilst in mum's care she would leave it until Dave got home, by which time the rash had flared up again.

My mum was a very large lady and I should have known that she found it difficult to get down onto the changing mat, she never said anything to me though.

*

When Emily was ten months old we took her out to the villa Dave's company owned, we had enjoyed it so much with my parents. Our dearest friends Monica and Mike came too. Monica was an M&S friend of many years and Emily's Godmother. It was easy having two extra pairs of hands to look after Emily as she was crawling into mischief by now. We showed Monica and Mike all the sights we had discovered the previous year with mum and dad and visited beautiful Guadalest again. I always thought of it as dad's perfect view. He had bought place mats there as a souvenir and looked at them and used them daily.

During that holiday with Monica and Mike we were able to swim every day; Emily was no stranger to the water as we had introduced her to swimming at just four months old. She really loved it.

The business of nappies and jars of baby food was a slight problem while we were there though. Friends had told me that these items were readily available and not to carry them with us. I found this to be untrue; there were nappies over there but not a patch on the ones we could get at home.

The same went for the baby food, Emily hated the brands we tried, she much preferred a chip in her hand or a piece of bread and washed it down with Dave's San Miguel!

She also enjoyed Spanish omelette and copious quantities of peanut butter. The supermarket we used didn't stock English sliced bread like they do today, we had to buy French sticks and scoop out the soft middle for Emily. When she was fed in the villa I had to tie her into the dinning chair with her reins, as we had no high chair, she slept in our room in a travel cot. Needless to say she survived and we all had a most relaxing holiday.

*

When Emily was two years old my darling Mam-mam died. She was 92 years old and had spent the last five years in a nursing home suffering from senile dementia. Before the disease really got a hold of her she had enjoyed seeing Emily go through the wonderful stages that toddler hood brings. I was always grateful that Mam-mam was blessed with a long life to witness us all in our relationships with each other. She was a true matriarch.

My mum tried to fit into that role after Mam-mam's death but she didn't get it quite right, she would be too moody and demanding and threaten to never see us again if she couldn't get her own way.

I by now, being a mother lion myself, stood up to her more and we clashed swords on more than one occasion. I once called her bluff and said if she felt like 'taking her ball in' she jolly well could, and see if I cared.

She continued to visit with a stony face for a little while and eventually thawed out and forgot about it. My dad just went along for the ride and pretty much did anything for a quiet life.

CHAPTER THIRTEEN

At this time we enjoyed taking Emily to all sort of lovely places, the seaside, amusement parks and zoos. One of the very best places we visited on a regular basis was called Sundown Pets Garden, it was a magical place of books and adventure and make believe. Children of all ages enjoyed it *especially* Dave and me! Sometimes mum and dad would come too. Dad's health was pretty stable and they had time on their hands.

I took her to toddler groups and had lots of pre-school friends round to play.

The winter of '93 we had a cold snap and I had had a very heavy cold, which turned to a chest infection. I had walked into town pushing the buggy with Emily wrapped up against the cold. I was going to see the doctor.

He prescribed some antibiotics so I stopped at the chemist to pick them up then walked home in the bitter cold, feeling really awful. That evening I was in a lot of pain in my chest. When I tried to lie down I found that I couldn't lie on my side, as the pain was so intense. It felt as if someone had put a brick under my arm.

Dave was very worried and called the doctor out. Our lady doctor was on call that night and when she saw me she admitted me to hospital with a suspected blood clot on my lung. It was all very frightening. Dave had to stay at home to be there for Emily so I had to call a taxi to take me into hospital.

When I got there I had all sorts of tests and was diagnosed with pneumonia. I spent the weekend in hospital where all the family came to visit me. I, at the time, didn't realise just how ill I was and was desperate to be home.

I was only going to be allowed home when my temperature returned somewhere near normal. I managed to get it down a bit by sticking my head out of the window!

When I did get home the worse was still to come, I was so weak that I was confined to bed for the next six weeks. The doctor came to see me every so often; in the first week home I was coughing up blood, I was really frightened. He said that it was quite normal and that I would be at least two months possibly three getting over the pneumonia and to take it easy. No one at the hospital had prepared me with what to expect.

My mum and Dave's mum took it in turns to have Emily during the day while Dave was at work. He would drop her off on his way to Corby and pick her up on the way home. Poor lad would then have to set about getting something for us all to eat and then bathe Emily and get her to bed.

I very slowly made progress, I couldn't believe that I had to tackle the stairs in three chunks with two rests in between where I'd always ran up them before.

Eventually I made a full recovery but my chest was weak, the following year I had a bout of pleurisy. I also had to make sure I had an influenza injection each year thereafter. A few weeks later and feeling much stronger my birthday was here again. Dave asked mum and dad to babysit and said he would take me out for a meal.

In reality Monica had arranged a surprise party for me at her house. There were about twelve guests and what a lovely gesture!

I think they all thought it was a close run thing and I could have lost my life. It was not uncommon for young people to die from pneumonia, I had been lucky.

*

When Emily was just turned three she started at a little private nursery I'd heard about from a friend. There were only twelve children there with two very dedicated teachers. They had been working with 3–5 year olds for a lot of years since having their own children and now grandchildren.

Emily went to nursery twice a week that first year and three times a week in her pre-school year. She will say to this day, that Mrs. Judge and Mrs. Snow were her best teachers ever!

She was already learning to read a little and to write a little and to really enjoy drawing. It would appear that she had inherited her dad's natural talent for art.

She was always a little reserved but did make friends.

She particularly enjoyed our times at the park. We only live a short walk from the central town park. In her pre-school years she enjoyed the sand pit and the paddling pool when the weather was good but loved the swings and slides and climbing frames all year round.

Emily was three years old, Lena was twenty years old. How had I managed to live for twenty whole years without being reunited with my first child, who was no longer a child? I was so saddened that I'd missed so much, especially as I was knowing first hand exactly what I had missed, experiencing it now with Emily.

It wasn't getting easier to come to terms with not having Lena in my life; there was a huge piece of my heart just waiting to be used by her.

*

For dad's birthday the previous year, Paul, Jayne and myself had clubbed together to send dad on a balloon flight (my idea). It was one of those things he'd always wanted to do. As the nicer weather was with us he had contacted the company and arranged a date to go up.

We all went along to watch the take off from somewhere near Rutland water. We tried to keep up with the balloon in our respective cars. Dave, Emily and I were in our car. Paul and Karen and their boys were in their car. Jayne was following in her car too and Mum was with her. We followed for as long as we could and then headed for home as it got near to Emily's bedtime. Then we waited to hear from mum and dad once they got home.

It was very late when the phone call came through but it was my brother. Paul rang from Leicester hospital. The balloon had landed in a ploughed field and on contact with the ground the basket had tipped over and all ten occupants had fallen onto dad. This was before balloon baskets were sectioned off into smaller areas. He had a broken pelvis and would be in hospital for a while. It was totally unbelievable!

He had six weeks in hospital where they discovered another side effect of the renal drugs had caused brittle bones. If he had known about the condition he might have thought more carefully about how dangerous ballooning was.

He would have a few months on crutches to contemplate it. I just felt so responsible for his injuries as it had been my idea in the first place.

Life just raced ahead and the weeks and the months flew by. It was one long round of mornings at nursery and afternoons at the park or meeting friend's to play. Toddler groups at church or at the library or mum and dad visiting. Getting ready to go to work and cycling there to do a three-hour shift.

Weekends were very busy too as I worked most of them. The Sunday trading laws had changed and M&S was open 10–4pm every Sunday now. I worked the Thursday late night every week and three out of four Saturdays and Sundays.

This did at least give me a weekend off every month. Those times were sacrosanct as family times and we usually did extra special things on those free weekends of mine.

Mum and dad still visited at least three times a week because they weren't at work and were at a loose end.

Dad had given up driving by this time and mum was the chauffeur, he'd given in gracefully when he realised that his sight was failing him.

It was sad really because driving was one of his passions.

We would often sit under our lovely willow tree in our garden if the weather was warm, while Emily played.

Mum hated the heat and it was all she could do to walk about. Dad was still keeping quite well but as he was closer to his 70th than his 60th he was becoming noticeably frail. The way he moved was slower and his hearing was deteriorating. Dad had always worn a hearing aid for as long as I could remember due to industrial deafness from the printing machines he'd worked around. Now he wore two hearing aids but when a lot of background noise was present he would shut himself off and let mum do all the talking.

He missed so much of the conversation it became a habit not to get involved from the outset. He was still a regular visitor to The Leicester General Hospital for check-ups and invariably went on his own. Mum seemed to do less and less these days.

*

I was feeling broody and wondered if Dave wanted to try for another baby so that Emily wouldn't be an only child. His response when I broached the subject was a very loud NO. He hadn't enjoyed the baby stage when there wasn't much interaction. He still remembered the sleepless nights we'd gone through together and didn't relish all that again. I told him I thought he was being totally selfish and should give it more thought.

By the beginning of October 1995 I was confirmed pregnant but Dave wasn't happy about the situation. It was too late to do anything about it and in his words "he'd have to grin and bear it."

We took a solemn walk around the park and tried to talk constructively about the forthcoming addition to the family. He decided that once the baby was older like Emily was now he would be fine with taking up the reins of fatherhood. I didn't want it to be like that, I really wanted him to be as happy as I was. I knew I couldn't change the situation but felt almost as miserable carrying this baby as I had been carrying Lena.

The baby was due in May 1996; Emily would be four and a half. She would be going to school in September of that same year. I just hoped the four months between the baby arriving and Emily going to school would be enough time to bond before she felt she was being pushed out. I now feel that a lot of Emily's later behaviour issues were due to jealousy.

*

My pregnancy was different to the two times before; I convinced myself that I was carrying differently some-how. I really longed for a boy this time, mainly for Dave's sake, and girls always looked like Lena. I stayed healthy even though I was always busy with a house to run and a pre_schooler to occupy. My life was fairly settled. The year wore on and Christmas and New Year came and went. The spring was upon us and I could count the weeks until the baby would be here.

*

We made an appointment to see the doctor to refer Dave for a vasectomy as soon as possible after the baby was born. Dave felt very strongly that this was definitely our last child.

When all was said and done I was 38 and Dave was 40, it was time to stop reproducing. The operation was booked for three months after the baby was due.

The time soon marched on until I was very close to my due date of the 9th May. I woke up very early on the

8th May with a bit of backache and a feeling of super heaviness under my huge bump. Again my waters didn't break so I had no inkling that I was in labour until the first dull contractions washed over me at about seven in the morning. I busied about all morning pottering and finding jobs to do until it was nearly lunchtime. It was already arranged earlier in the week that mum and dad would come over to have fish and chips for lunch. It was mum's favourite meal of all time and nothing would keep her away.

We rang them and said that Dave was home because the baby was on its way. The five of us (Mum, Dad, Emily Dave and myself) sat down to our fish and chip lunch. Me clutching the edge of the table every so often as a contraction swept over me. This really put my dad off his dinner; he looked more uncomfortable as the meal wore on. He probably thought that if I'd left it a bit too late he would be called upon use his first aid skills to deliver his own grandchild!

When I decided I hadn't got any more room for the dinner we were on our way to the maternity unit once more.

This time I didn't have any gas and air and had a wonderfully natural birth. We stayed in the beautifully decorated Victoria Suite, which had an en-suite bathroom. We played our favourite music and basically I enjoyed the whole experience. I felt I finally knew what I was doing after two practice runs, I felt in control.

The midwife I had was superb, every time there was the slightest notion of a scream coming from me she said "NO!! Helen! Channel that energy into pushing, come on now!"

Dave stayed with me and every time a big contraction came I pulled down on his back. At 3.30pm. Charlotte Amanda Hudson made a very lusty entrance into the world. She weighed in at 7 lb. 13 oz. and I didn't have stitches or any problems at all.

I only had one night in hospital during which time Dave and Emily visited.

Emily seemed to be a bit bemused by the whole affair and nursed Charlotte tentatively. The next morning Emily and Dave came to fetch us home. Later that day Mum and Dad came to visit us all and the camcorder again recorded the happy event.

Charlotte was born with a birthmark on her right temple and we realised that she was going to be a 'Granddad's girl'. My dad had recently had a large melanoma removed from exactly the same spot on his right temple. Over the previous twelve months he had had various growths removed from his arms and face. The doctors said that the drugs he had been taking for many years played a part in the resulting melanomas, the sun playing a big part too.

Charlotte was a contented baby but I only managed to breastfeed her for the first month, again because I tried to be 'super-mum'. I didn't stay still long enough for milk production to get fully under-way.

Once she was bottle-fed she really thrived. We took endless videos of the girls but looking back at them, without realising it, we had pushed Emily out to get shots of the newborn. Emily would come right up to the camcorder and say, "Can you see me daddy?" Dave would say, Yes darling but just move to the side so we can see Charlotte" and things like that.

Those early days were where the jealousy first started. Even though the girls get on quite well there is an element of 'green eye' to their relationship. They each think the other is more fairly treated and better loved, especially Emily.

In September of '96 Emily started school and enjoyed it from the start. My days were spent doing all the toddler groups and meeting with other mums and pre-schoolers as I had done with Emily. The school was near to the park so on good days we could pick Emily up from school and spend a pleasant hour at the park before coming home to get the tea ready.

Charlotte and I would often go to the park after dropping Emily off at school in the morning too. Mum and Dad were still very frequent visitors. We used to go to their house on a Wednesday and spend the whole day there until it was time to get Ems from school. I really enjoyed those early years with both my girls, they were very special times.

Early in the New Year Dave lost his dad, he had been poorly towards the end of '96 and had gone into hospital with pneumonia. He died on the 4th January and the funeral was on my birthday (15th). We put on a little spread at our house for anyone that wanted to come back after the Crematorium Service. Hilda was alone now. I couldn't begin to imagine what she was feeling, my heart ached for her. My love for her would grow and grow.

CHAPTER FOURTEEN

Lena was 24 years old and still there was no word from her. It was no less painful now than when I first came home from hospital after having her. I had always assumed that as soon as she turned eighteen she would want to make contact. If only she knew that she had two 'full' sisters and a mum and dad who were still together. I started to get impatient and wondered if there was anything else I could do. Bear in mind this is before the days of the Internet.

I saw a television programme called 'The Forgotten Mothers' about women just like me who'd had similar experiences, teenage pregnancies and the adoption law as it stood. It was a one-way street, adopted people could seek their birth parents but it couldn't be initiated from the other way round. At the end of the programme there were details of a leaflet to send off for. I sent for the leaflet and then had several phone numbers and agencies to get in touch with.

I spent hours on the phone chatting to various very sympathetic people. One of the agencies had a support group, meeting monthly in Peterborough so I started to attend. I went along the first time not really knowing what to expect. There were about twenty people sat around a huge table talking about their experiences,

I discovered that most of them were adopted people trying to find their birth mothers.

It was all so sad, so many people having difficulty finding the ones they were seeking. I was more than willing to talk to the group about my experiences and hoped it would help them to see the other side of the coin. In a bizarre way it helped me too, simply being able to talk. I carried on going to the meetings for about two years. I met different people every time I went and shared my sad tale.

I talked with adopted people who were very bitter about being 'given away' and hated their birth mothers without even knowing the circumstances of their adoption. Was this why I had not heard from my own dear Lena? I met adopted people who had a deep and passionate longing to find their birth mother. Why oh why couldn't it be like that for Lena and me?

During that time I received a monthly newsletter with some happy endings in it. An adopted person had been re-united with a birth mother and found they had dozens more members of a previously unknown family. This gave me hope. The statistics showed that a lot of adopted people waited until their adoptive parents died before thinking about finding their roots. A lot of the happy endings in the newsletters were of reunions that were short lived. The search had taken so many years that the birth mother was infirm or died soon after. They probably only had a few months to catch up a whole lifetime. Please God, this was not going to be how it was for me.

My name and address details were with every agency possible and I also left a letter for Lena telling her about the reasons for her adoption and what she could look forward to in us, her mum and dad and two full sisters.

It was very strange to learn that when adopted people and their birth parents were reunited they would have counselling every step of the way. This also applied to anyone who was affected by the reunion.

There wasn't a bit of counselling to be had when I could have most done with it. When Lena was taken from me I could have benefited so much from talking to someone.

Twenty-four years later, the NORCAP meetings were helping but it left me feeling even more useless. Was I destined to be a doddery old lady with senile dementia before I would have my one and only wish come true?

*

At the end of '97 dad would be celebrating his 70th birthday. I took my mind off things by planning a big surprise party at my house. I invited all the family and tracked down some old work colleagues of his. I ordered a limousine to pick mum and dad up from their house to bring them to the party. I ordered a huge cake and planned the buffet. I chose not to tell mum about any of it so that she wouldn't have to lie to dad, it would be as much a surprise for her as for him.

As the date for the party got nearer I was a whirling dervish. On the actual party day things went really smoothly. The buffet was laid out and all the guests arrived in plenty of time. It just remained for me to go over to mum and dad's house to collect them. They thought they were coming for a simple roast dinner with the four of us!

Emily came in the limousine with me and we pretended we were celebrities and waved at everyone like the Queen does all the way back to our house.

When we got to Stanground mum and dad's faces were a picture on seeing the limousine, but of course it didn't end there, there were about fifty guests waiting for them at my house. There were banners and balloons and old photographs around the house. Dad had a fantastic time and so did mum, they couldn't believe the amount of trouble I had gone to. It gave me so much pleasure to do that for them.

That year Christmas could have been an anticlimax after so much planning and activity and partying. But with little ones it would always be a magical time, and it was.

Next it was my turn for a milestone birthday, I was forty years old and how had that happened? I asked Dave not to do a surprise party, as I hadn't got over the shock of the small party they'd arranged after my illness. I did still celebrate it though; I did the catering myself and had an open house affair. It was very enjoyable.

I decided that the monthly NORCAP meetings had lost their original purpose and so stopped going. The constant soul searching had left me quite raw and of course no nearer to my own reunion with Lena. My details were there for her and a letter so I just had to resign myself to more waiting. I still received the newsletters and sometimes there would be a similar story with a happy ending leaving me feeling elated. Other times there would be a sad story, a reunion left too late and that left me feeling deflated.

One Sunday afternoon I left the girls with Dave and went over to have a 'chat' with mum and dad. They knew something was afoot when I arrived on my own. We got a cup of tea and all sat down, it came out in a torrent. "Well, you know that I'm a big girl now, I'm forty years old. When I was sixteen you made decisions for me, but from now on I make my own decisions. If Lena gets in touch at this address I will be the one calling the tune, not either of you. I will decide who she meets, when she meets and if she meets. I don't blame you for how things were dealt with at the time. I am in charge of how things will be from now on."

It was chin on chest time for my parents; they were very shocked that after all this time that I could open all the old wounds. I was forcing them to talk about things, it was so long overdue. We talked for quite a long time and dad cried because he said he had carried a lot of guilt for so long.

He wanted to make it up to me by hiring a private detective to try to locate Lena. I said that it wasn't as simple as that and we had to consider that there were other people involved who might get hurt.

Our side of the story was very neat and tidy because Dave and I were still together and we had Emily and Charlotte. For Lena's side there were her adoptive parents, it was unfair to rock their boat.

We just had to wait until Lena was ready to meet with us. If I am perfectly honest it frightened me to think that events could be forced. I wanted them to happen as was laid out somewhere in the grand scheme of things.

I felt somewhat relieved that for the first time in history my parents had faced up to something without it becoming a heated argument and eventual falling out. I had forced them to be adults for the first time in their lives! That was the time when they could have given me the photo and letter, but still chose not to!

Later that year (August) Dave and I had a shock waiting for us. It was during the summer holidays so both girls were playing in the garden and mum and dad had called in for a coffee. The phone rang and it was Dave. He said, "Sorry to ring you darling but I've just been told I'm being made redundant." I replied, "Just come straight home but please, please drive carefully." I came off the phone and promptly burst into floods of tears. Mum and dad were there and able to console me. What on earth were we going to do?

Emily was six and Charlie was two, how would we support the family now? Dad said not to worry too much as something would come along.

Dave came home a broken man. Twenty years of loyal service meant nothing.

When I went to work on the following Thursday I told my Line Manager what had happened and she was able to give me full-time work for as long as I needed it. Dave stayed at home and looked after the girls and I went back to full-time work the next Monday morning. We were setting up a new store in the Queensgate Centre and I was in charge of organising the warehouse, it was heavy, demanding work.

The first hard day back at work had finally finished and I wearily cycled home. When I got home a lovely hot meal was waiting for me and Dave had very kindly set up the ironing board and iron for me! I soon put him right and said that as he was a house-husband the ironing was now his domain. I gave him a quick training session and then left him to it while the girls and I had a lovely long bath. This was the real world. When school started back in September he took Emily there then went to the park with Charlie, he did the shopping and some housework but his confidence had taken an awful knock.

I ended up working for six more weeks before Dave secured a Christmas job with M&S and we swapped roles again.

Dave had an idea that he wanted to work for himself. He said he never wanted to go through that feeling of helplessness again and being self-employed would ensure that everything he put into his work would be for us alone. He wanted to be a Painter and Decorator. All the Graphic Design jobs were computer based and his lack of knowledge in that area and his age were against him. He was forty-two. I felt very bitter that Blaze had not kept him up to date with developments in the business. They had left him at his drawing board when so much was happening with the technology side of things.

The idea of Dave being a painter and decorator didn't sit well with me either. He was very good at this particular craft as our own house and both sets of parents' houses would testify, but could he make a living out of it?

I worried that the perfectionist that he was wouldn't be able to work fast enough to actually earn enough money to support us. We had a friend in the business and went over to his house to discuss the ins and outs of it all. Graham was one of those chums from the Devon adventure and had been made redundant from an engineering company some fifteen years earlier. His partner Terri did the bookkeeping side of things, which would fall to me if we went ahead with this idea. Dave was even more enthusiastic once he'd been over to see Graham.

We saw in the New Year of '99 with some hopes and dreams and a lot of worry. I made an appointment to see an Accountant and he outlined how I should set up the bookkeeping side of things. Dave's contract with

M&S finished at the end of January. He got some of his initial business from M&S people he got to know during his time there.

On the 15th February 1999 he put on his first white overall and set out into the world as a Painter and Decorator. We were to happily find out that when one door closes another one opens.

CHAPTER FIFTEEN

Dave worked so hard and his reputation grew. He had a 'fan club' at M&S as people clamoured to be next to have their rooms 'done' by him. It was amazing, we were on our way!

Everyone loved the fact that he was such a perfectionist; the standard of work was exceptional. I was never so pleased to be wrong about something in my entire life. One job led to another and to another.

Parents of Emily's school friends would join the list of people wanting quotes and consequently decorating done. Little girls in the playground would be heard to say, "Emily's daddy is doing my bedroom next!" As some sort of one-upmanship would take hold and baby pink was the order of the day.

I was still doing my few hours at M&S. By the time we realised that we'd been in business six months and had survived it all, it all seemed rather natural.

That summer we were very fortunate to have a holiday. Hilda had entered a competition and had won a holiday for four, all-inclusive, down in Somerset. She very kindly gave it to us and Dave was able to get a well-earned rest. We all enjoyed the break too. When we got home it was straight back to work for Dave as he was very busy.

I celebrated 25 years service with M&S. The company really spoiled employees when they stayed loyal for that amount of time. Dave and I were treated to two nights in a London hotel. We stayed at the Cumberland Hotel near Marble Arch. After the presentation at Head Office there was a cocktail party followed by a West End show. Jayne came to look after the girls for us and took them to school and nursery respectively.

There were also five work colleagues from the Peterborough store celebrating 25 years service with me.

The hotel was fantastic, Dave and I had never stayed anywhere quite so posh. The presentation was awe-inspiring as the board sat and sang the praises of the room full of loyal employees.

There were over two hundred people celebrating 25 years service and five people celebrating 40 years of service. I chose for my gift from the company a 22 carat gold bangle and matching earrings. These were presented to me, when my turn came, in an engraved box. It was all very thrilling,

The cocktail party was unlike anything we'd ever been to. The canapés came out on silver platters in an endless stream, as did the champagne. It was a very heady night. We met Stella Riddington, of MI6 there. Next we were transferred by coach to our respective theatres. I had chosen to go to see Miss Saigon; it was a magical show and the likes I've never seen before or since. The show finished a ten-year run later that same year so it seemed even more special.

The next day Dave and I walked across Hyde Park to Knightsbridge and we went shopping in Harrods. Something else I'd never done before. It was a fabulous two days in London. I still wear my bangle and earrings with pride many years later.

*

At the end of '99 Mum would celebrate her 70th birthday. I told her I would do a party for her but it obviously couldn't be a surprise. I did it very much along the same lines as Dad's party two years previously. I invited more or less the same people and had the same sort of cake and even hired the limousine again. Nonetheless for that she had a perfectly enjoyable time.

Christmas came round again and the Millennium Night was fast approaching, we chose to see the new century in with our neighbours. We had a brilliant party with fireworks at midnight and both girls stayed up too. It had been several years since we'd seen the New Year in with my parents especially since dad gave up driving. We had to make do with a phone call.

Dad by this time was starting to have more hospital appointments than hot dinners. The melanomas were still causing him a lot of discomfort and to add to his problems his kidney was showing early signs of malfunction. What with the failing kidney, the loss of hearing and eyesight, the brittle bones and the melanomas, life for dad was less than 'quality' now.

We had to keep reminding ourselves that he had had an extra twenty-five years with us. All this was due to the advances in medical science.

September 2000 Charlotte started infants' school, Emily was by now at junior school. It all seemed wrong as I worked most weekends and the girls were in school all week.

I was doing a cleaning job, two hours on a Monday and two hours on a Friday for a fiver an hour. I was also a Dinner Lady at Emily's school every day. I carried on with these other jobs and M&S for a while. I was very disappointed that M&S couldn't offer term-time work which was what I wanted. My 28 years of service counted for nothing. I even wrote to the Chairman, to no avail.

In time a Teaching Assistant post came up at Charlie's school and I was successful in my application.

Eventually I was able to give up M&S and the cleaning job and the dinner lady job. I worked 19 hours in school and had the same holidays as the girls, it was ideal. I loved the work, it was very rewarding, I had training and worked in the reception unit with autistic children.

Dad's health was deteriorating and I was shocked at how frail he was starting to look. Eventually his second kidney failed so it was decided that it would have to be removed.

Things had come on a lot since the early days of home dialysis and he was fitted with a new system that operated with a bag. An 'exchange' was done four times a day and used the peritoneal membrane instead of a kidney. Mum and Dad had the training to enable them to manage it at home.

It was a drip system whereby dad had to sit whilst the contents of the bag went into him into a small tap fitted into his abdomen. After a while the fluid did the work of the kidney and he then had to remove it the same way. I didn't understand how it worked but it did.

He had also recently had another large melanoma removed from his right eyelid. This had left him with a 'V' shaped piece missing from that eyelid, even when it was closed you could see a little bit of his eyeball.

After only a short while they were getting on quite confidently with the new system and dad seemed to rally round a bit.

November 2000 dad was 74 years old. Another month and Christmas was upon us again. Emily enjoyed her tenth and Charlie enjoyed her fifth Christmas. Nanny and Granddad spent the day with us as normal and it was lovely to all be together. Another New Year to see in next week!

I asked if mum and dad would be staying up to see the New Year in at home and should I ring at midnight? Mum said that as it was just an ordinary year, not a millennium as last year had been, they probably wouldn't stay up. I said I would leave the phone call until New Years Day.

*

What we ended up doing on New Years Day was hospital visiting. Dad had managed to catch his eye with one of the scratchy old melanomas on his arm. Because he had a partial eyelid the wart had lacerated his eye and it had become infected. It looked a real mess but at least he was in the best place to get it seen to. His hospitalisation meant that his kidney paraphernalia had to go with him. Mum had to do the bag changes for him, as the nurses on duty weren't trained renal nurses. They were too busy anyway.

They pumped him full of antibiotics to try to zap the infection. This was an unfortunate thing because the drugs he was already on and too large a dose of antibiotic caused a chemical reaction that made him hallucinate. He fell out of bed and hurt himself, taking all the skin off his forearm. They got that patched up and then carried on with the incorrect dose of antibiotic. This time he thought he was under threat and he ran from the ward and down two flights of stairs to the reception area before being challenged. We could never understand where he got the strength from as without the cocktail of drugs he was so frail.

He was in hospital for the whole of January and the infection was still very much in evidence. Mum was getting very tired visiting every day. I suggested she visit every other day and I visited every evening once Dave was home from work. I was able to help dad with his bag changes. Paul and Jayne were able to do their bit too. We saw more of each other at his bedside than we had done for a long time. Sometimes dad would be asleep but Paul and I would have some good conversations, likewise with Jayne. I especially enjoyed seeing Jayne as we were very close.

The consultant who was seeing dad for the treatment of the infected eye was saddened to have to tell us that the only way to go forward and get rid of the infection was to remove the eye. This was all a bit shocking. Dad's debilitated renal system wasn't helping the situation and that was another reason he just couldn't fight the infection. Dad took it all in his stride and went ahead with yet another operation.

I will never forget how brave he was, waiting to go down to have that eye removed. He knew the operation was going to be done under a local anaesthetic. He was too weak to cope with a general anaesthetic. I went to visit him that morning knowing that he was going to have his eye removed, he just sat there as if he was going to have nothing more than one of his melanomas removed. He'd got so used to going under the knife.

He came back from the operating theatre fairly quickly that morning and we all visited him later that evening.

The operation had been a success he just had to get on with getting better now. Dad had spent the whole of the year so far in hospital (6 weeks) and during that time I had taken the girls to see him. I had explained to them exactly what Granddad was going to have done and then told them that it was OK to go and see him. They were quite used to hospitals as we all were. Granddad managed to do a really good impression of a pirate with his eye patch on and made everyone laugh.

I remember after one of his very early kidney transplants he had us all rolling with laughter. The Consultant Surgeon had come to my dad's bedside with an entourage of students. He explained to the students the procedures that had taken place and how the patient would be monitored for fluid input and output for several days to make sure the new kidney was functioning properly. After some question and answer time between them the Consultant asked, "Is there anything you wish to ask us Mr. Crooks?" Dad said with a deadpan face, "Yes, will I be able to play the piano?" The Consultant replied, "Of course you'll be able to play the piano". "O great!" said dad, "I never could before!"

This was a small window when dad was feeling up beat and positive about things. It would be soon after this that he started to feel quite poorly again.

Removing the infected eye had only given him a little respite because the poison was still present in his system. I was visiting every night and wasn't seeing any improvement at all.

The Consultant spoke to me one day in his office and told me that it was really only a matter of time before dad's body would start to close down completely. It was heartbreaking news but it was true that his poor chopped about flesh couldn't take much more.

I once sat on his hospital bed and he said, "You know, there's just one final thing I have to do, don't you?" He knew how ill he was and was asking for permission to die.

CHAPTER SIXTEEN

It was a very stressful time for us all. One evening there was just Paul, Jayne and myself around Dad's bedside and he was snoozing whilst we all chatted.

Paul had been in to see the consultant earlier in the day and I wondered what he had said this time. When I asked what he had said Paul suddenly turned on me and said, "For the first time in my life I know something that you don't know, I can't tell you how good that feels. Whatever I've ever said or done has been because you've said to do it. You're a bossy cow and I'm sick of it. So this time I know something that you don't know!" Well, you could have knocked me down with a feather. My dearest brother whom I loved with all of my heart was telling me how it was for him. I always knew that I was a strong character, and a control freak at that, due to my past but Jesus, I didn't deserve to be spoken to like that. I'd had be made of steel to have gone through what I'd been through. I didn't realise that Paul had all this pent up anger inside him that was caused by me. We were all pretty stressed; we knew we were losing our Father.

He carried on with, "You had to have mum and dad every Christmas, every Easter, every Fathers day, Every Mothers day, and birthdays, you never gave anyone else a chance." This was total garbage because if he'd really wanted to invite mum and dad he would have gone ahead and done so.

It was totally unfair, let's be honest he only had to ask and they would have gone there. He always waited until they had been invited to me and must have then thought, "Ah, mum and dad are at Helen's this year again, well never mind maybe next year eh?" I never once in my life heard him say, "Do you think that mum and dad could come to us for a change?" He liked the idea that they were always at mine; it meant he could get on with his life.

Paul was forty years old but was acting like a moody teenager. It came from nowhere and it was as if his whole lifes worth of injustices were all down to me, his elder bossy sister.

I was just so shocked and hurt; all I'd wanted to know was what the Consultant had said. To find out that Paul felt so much hatred towards me was more than I could stand.

I suddenly couldn't breathe the same air as him and started off down the ward towards the exit and the car park.

As a parting shot and because I was livid about the way my brother saw me I had the last words with, "you are totally f***ing out of order!" This was spat out half way down the ward before I fled, sobbing, to my car.

I arrived home in a total state, Dave didn't know how to console me much less find out what had caused my distress.

Jayne turned up shortly after me and said that she couldn't believe what she had witnessed. She told Dave, in a nutshell what had happened. I was so desperate to receive an apology from Paul that a little later I phoned him at home.

I could only get as far as Karen who had obviously been given a different account of events. We spent several minutes shrieking at each other then slamming the phone down, only to be phoned back with more of the same. It was a total impasse; Dave refused to get involved even though Karen had joined forces with her partner. Jayne didn't want too fight in my corner even though she had witnessed it all.

I felt very bitter about the way I'd been treated but could discuss it no more. From then on if Paul was visiting dad when I arrived at the hospital I would go away and come back later. If I was there first and he arrived I'd say I was going anyway and beat a hasty retreat.

Usually we just managed to miss each other. Dad knew something was wrong and said as much to mum, he could sense an atmosphere but he hadn't witnessed the fracas so he never knew the details.

Mum spent a lot of times after that trying to persuade us to make up. We were unable to ever be back on the same footing as we had been on before the argument. I never knew what Paul had told mum but I told her I would never speak to him again.

*

It was decided that dad would be nursed at home with district nurses calling three times a day. Mum would be able to do the bag changes for him. A single bed was bought and set up in the dining room (the old dialysis room) and the nurses visited mum to make themselves known.

Everything was in place for dad to be transferred home. He actually managed to be there for a mere two days before things started to go horribly wrong with his renal bag system.

Each bag was checked for infection and this time he had produced a really cloudy bag the likes of which mum had never seen. She had very quickly got the doctor to come out and an ambulance was called. Mum rang Jayne and I in a panic and we both arrived at the house at the same time. Our worst fear was of peritonitis.

It was snowing quite hard that day and the ambulance arrived; mum asked if one of us would go with him and I said I would. Knowing my relationship with Dave, I couldn't imagine seeing him being whisked away in an ambulance without me being as close as I could get.

Mum however, for whatever reasons, didn't want to go in the ambulance. Jayne followed behind in her car, she brought mum with her. As soon as Paul could be contacted he joined us there. I'd only ever been in an ambulance when we had our accident in the Reliant, that time I sat up and had a short journey to the District Hospital.

This time it was a blue light dash to Leicester General Hospital where dad had all his renal appointments. The blue light was flashing and the siren was wailing. Looking through the front windscreen, it was as if they were taking a hair dryer to any traffic and blowing it away. Dad was in a very poor state and seemed to be slipping in and out of consciousness for the whole journey. My main concern was that I would join him on the other stretcher after suffering a heart attack because I was so scared that we wouldn't make it in time. The crew were absolutely brilliant, they spoke to dad even though he wasn't conscious and calmed me throughout the whole journey.

We arrived at the hospital in no time at all and then all hell broke loose.

The medical staffs were running hither and yon, somehow I managed to keep up and get to a ward where all sorts of tests were carried out.

Jayne and mum arrived after what seemed an eternity and then Paul arrived. Our very worst nightmare had come true, Dad was diagnosed with peritonitis. This was serious stuff and we all feared for his life.

The nursing staff were fantastic and made him really comfortable and soon had him stable. The only thing to do was to head back to Peterborough and visit again the next day. This we did for several days but dad never gained full consciousness.

I was trying to keep several juggling balls in the air at the same time, my work, the house and the family. Dave stepped into the breech so that I could drive mum to Leicester or go with Jayne to visit dad. When Paul and I met we only spoke when absolutely necessary.

On one of the evenings I was holding dad's hand and I thought to communicate with him. I asked him to squeeze my hand if he was in pain. He responded with quite a firm squeeze.

I was then on a mission to get him some more pain relief. A morphine drip was set up for him and we had to resign ourselves that he wasn't coming home. I couldn't think about that, I just wanted his years of hospitals and operations to come to an end. Even though he'd asked permission to die some weeks before, I hadn't told anyone but Dave that dad had said those things.

Each time we visited, dad looked more ill. He had been in Peterborough hospital since New Year's Day and now these few days in Leicester hospital. We were now in the first week of March.

I asked dad again if he was in pain and he responded with a very feeble squeeze but it was enough of a squeeze for me.

I went to a male nurse and told him if he didn't get my dad some more morphine or something, I was going to put a pillow over my dad's face and suffocate him. He was very sympathetic and managed to calm me down with an explanation of the morphine pump that dad was fitted to. The morphine was continuous there was nothing else they could do. We drove back to Peterborough in a daze again.

The next day mum had a phone call at about eleven in the morning to say that dad had taken a turn for the worse and could the family get there as soon as possible. Jayne had picked mum up and then came to get me out of work (my head Teacher was very understanding). We did the mercy dash to Leicester yet again. Paul was already there as he had been working near Bedford, which is closer. He looked very relieved that we had made it in time.

They had moved dad into a side room and he looked lifeless. His skin was very waxy in appearance and his one good eye was no longer bright blue and twinkly as it had been in life but very dull, as if the light had been switched off inside him.

We had arrived at about one o'clock in the afternoon and the three of us just stood around the bedside drinking tea and watching him. There were uncomfortable silences where we didn't want to talk about dad as if he was no longer there but in reality he was no longer there.

As it was March so it got dark quite early and mum started to make noises that she wanted to be away home. I'm convinced the soaps that she watched were more important than being there!

I wanted to stay to make sure dad didn't die alone but didn't want to be the cause of another hospital bed scene. We all decided that we would have one more cup of tea and then see how things were.

When the tea tray was brought in it contained lovely little bone china cups and saucers with dinky little handles. We had a bit of a laugh about them as Paul's great hands made the cups look even smaller. It's not the sort of cup a carpenter drinks out of sticking his pinkie in the air!

We then started to include dad in our conversation. We each in turn said loving things in his ears and reassured him that we would look after mum and for him to get on with what he was supposed to be doing. We reassured him several times and wondered what he was waiting for. For some reason after talking to him for the last time I took out both hearing aids. Within a matter of a few seconds he had slipped away.

It was 4pm on 9th March 2001. It was the end of an era. Jayne and mum drove back in one car and to show solidarity I accompanied Paul in his van back to Peterborough. We only made small talk and it was very strained. We all arrived back at mum's house and took in the enormity of what had really happened. Mum insisted she would be OK to sleep in the house on her own and told us all to go home. We all checked her by ringing and arranged to start funeral arrangements the next day.

As dad had died in Leicester Paul and I had to collect the death certificate from the registrar in Leicester. The next step was to visit the funeral directors and we all went together. It was a surreal situation talking about coffins and music and number of cars, Mum held up really well.

Once Dad was transferred to the Co-Op chapel of rest in Peterborough we were able to go to see him. I remembered the trauma I had suffered when I'd been to see my uncle Maurice there, and worried it wouldn't be a good experience.

I need not have worried because Dad really did look at peace. I went to visit him several times in the eight days he was there and took comfort from those visits.

I sat and chatted about all sorts of things. I realised several years later I that I didn't take him to task over throwing me out on the street twenty-six years previously. I could have done that, while he for once didn't answer back or say, "Do as I say not as I do."

The Vicar came to see Mum one evening and the three of us were there too. We all had input into dad's eulogy because we admired his bravery so much. It was still unbelievable that he had gone.

There were reams of forms to fill out and it worried mum greatly. I was the one working the fewest number of hours so naturally I helped with as much as I could.

Dad had specified that he didn't want any black at his funeral. I personally wore a red suit for the occasion and it felt just right.

The cup of tea and sandwich after the crematorium was at my house at mum's request. I offered to do it and she was really grateful because she said we'd had so many lovely occasions there. I felt that Emily and

Charlotte were too young to attend the funeral (ten and five respectively) so I arranged that they stay with a friend of mine after they finished school that day. It wasn't that they couldn't cope with it but seeing so many people crying would have been difficult for them.

The day of the funeral arrived and we all gathered at mum's house. We made small talk but it was an eerie atmosphere. Eventually the hearse arrived and we came outside to go to our cars to follow.

This was where I completely lost it for a couple of minutes until Jayne consoled me and gave me the strength to carry on. Later on our roles would reverse and she would need me to console her. We were even closer than we'd ever been in our shared grief. Following the hearse was just so bizarre and Mum held up really well on the journey. Dad's dearest friend, my Godfather was out of the country when the funeral was held but sent a wonderful letter for the vicar to read out.

I had arranged the music with another uncle. Dad loved Glenn Miller music so we went in to the crematorium to '*Little Brown Jug*' and came out to '*In the Mood.*'

It was a relief all round when it was over and done. We all came back to the house and had tea and sandwiches and cake. I remember there being laughter there.

Once it was over Paul and I had no reason to see each other again and I know that suited me fine. I'm sure he felt the same or he would have contacted me.

Some weeks later I had to remind mum that I had lost my father when she was the grieving widow, without any regard for my feelings. When she was still very low many weeks later I was quite harsh with her and reminded her that dad wasn't a saint but a mortal man who had bullied and hurt her on occasion, as he had done with all of us. She had him up on a pedestal; he was bound to tumble down.

I missed him so much, he wasn't perfect and none of us are. There was a real void where he had been and I didn't think I would ever feel happy again. Sure as life goes on so the stages of grief pass, the anger, the questions of faith, the loneliness and eventually a feeling that it is all part of the grand scheme of things. Sooner or later you realise you've moved on slightly and are able to move on some more.

The legacy he left was that of a very brave man doing the best he knew how.

CHAPTER SEVENTEEN

We fell into a pattern of having Mum over most Sundays because in her words, "It's the loneliest day of the week." I always made a point of visiting Mum at her home at least once a week if only for a short time, taking the girls with me.

I would hear a joke or an anecdote and think, "I must ring Dad and tell him that tonight", only to realise that he was gone.

A fresh wave of grief would sweep over me and I would think I was back to square one. You know that as you get older it's all par for the course and grief can strike at any time. It can be a sound, a smell, a piece of music or thinking of a particular memory or place that would trigger it.

The Hudson family had spent the previous three years holidaying in Dartmouth in Devon. We loved the area and it was an ideal opportunity to see Peter, Jenny and Gemma and catch up with them without being on top of them.

We had a favourite beach (Blackpool Sands) where the girls could play on the beautiful golden sand and swim in the sea. They also loved to splash around in their inflatable boat on the small freshwater lake there.

The summer of '01 when Mum was so recently widowed I said to Dave that I didn't want to go so far away that year. We looked at cottages nearer to home and found a delightful one in a sleepy village in Norfolk. The village is called Aldborough and boasts one of the largest village greens in the country. Quintessentially English when a game of cricket is in progress. The village is fifteen minutes from Sheringham and a similar distance from Cromer, a really lovely part of Norfolk.

The cottage sleeps five so we asked Mum if she'd like to come with us. She agreed when we said she need only stay a few days and then Dave would drive her home. This is what happened and when Dave brought her back to Peterborough he returned with his mum to stay with us for a few days.

We four had a whole two weeks there so we still had some great family time together. We took both mums out for meals and sightseeing and the days at the beach were idyllic. We travelled round the Norfolk coast to Sea Paling to find the best beach. We loved it so much that we have been back every Easter since and a couple of times in the summer as well.

Each time we go back to Aldborough we get to know more local people. Dave and I would dearly love to retire to the area when the time comes.

Dave's business was still thriving, the girls were happy and settled at their schools and I was still enjoying my job very much. Life was on an even keel. The years were just flying by, Dave was 45, I was 43, Lena was 27, Emily was 10 and Charlotte 5.

*

The first Christmas was difficult without Dad at the table and a very emotional time. The 'firsts' of everything were painful because if it required a card the greeting would say 'love from Mum'. I would light a candle for him on his birthday, Fathers day and the anniversary of his death.

Soon another year would dawn and in 2002 Dave and I looked forward to celebrating our Silver Wedding anniversary. I was very sad that Dad had missed it by one year but glad that he knew that Dave and I would be together forever.

We planned an open house affair with a running BBQ. Mum, Jayne and her partner Ray were invited along with all the neighbours and many friends.

Paul had called in briefly with a rose bush called 'Silver Wedding Day' earlier that week and had wished us a happy anniversary. We didn't tell him about the open house. We still weren't on speaking terms.

All the birthdays within our respective families had been acknowledged with money or gift vouchers in the cards but nothing more. Every time we had to be together to exchange these cards conversation had been stilted. Soon we moved on to just posting the cards and not calling at all. Five years would pass before we spoke properly again.

The day of our silver wedding celebrations was a really enjoyable one tinged with sadness. I felt I couldn't go overboard with things, as mum hadn't been there on our big day. I didn't want to appear to rub her nose in it. She spent the whole day with us and saw most people that came with good wishes and gifts, everyone knowing that she had not been with us twenty-five years ago. Dad and she had always said our marriage wouldn't last, so it was nice to prove them wrong.

We also celebrated the event with two weeks in Rhodes with the girls at a beautiful hotel right on the beach. It was our first experience of an all-inclusive holiday. What a treat, especially for a busy mum like me. We hired a car for seven of the fourteen days and explored the ancient ruins and found wonderful beaches. The rest of the time we lazed by our hotel pool or on the hotel beach, fetching drinks or refreshments whenever we needed them. The girls went to kids clubs and Dave and I could be alone enjoying our second honeymoon, or even first honeymoon!

It was such a fantastic holiday we saved up and had another 'big' holiday two years later, all-inclusive again. We were very lucky to be in a financial position to be able to do this; it was all down to Dave's incredible hard work.

The twenty-five years of marriage had seen ups and downs like any relationship, often minor arguments would erupt into major traumas. The making up afterwards was always good and things would go along on an even keel for a while until the next blip. I think we both knew that the commitment we had made to each other was pretty solid, we just tested it every once in a while. Dave, always the placid one would usually be the one wanting to make up first.

During the summer holidays of 2003 I was laying in bed one morning, reading with the girls, one either side of me. I suddenly started to tell them about what had happened with Dave and me and Lena's arrival some 29 years previously.

I wanted them to be able to take as much on board as they could and then come back with any questions whenever they felt ready. Emily in particular realised that she wasn't the first-born but was still the eldest in a bizarre turn of fate.

The main thing was that Charlotte was just about old enough to understand the situation (seven) but my immediate concern was for Emily (12) who was almost the same age as I had been when I started going out with Dave.

It was the sex talk with a real background story to warn of the dangers of teenage pregnancy. Charlotte was the one to be the most animated about having another sister and would talk very openly about it, hoping that Lena would hurry up and find us all soon.

The next time we saw my Mum Charlotte said, "Nanny, I've got an older sister." At first mum thought she was referring to the doll she was carrying and said, "oh, lovely Charlotte."

"No, I mean Lena and she's coming to find us all soon, isn't she?" replied Charlotte. Nanny at this point nearly choked on her false teeth and looked at me as if I'd taken leave of my senses. I said, "Well, I didn't set out to tell them on any particular day but it suddenly seemed the right time to do it."

I wanted to be able to talk to my daughters' about anything and hoped we could go through their teenage years without major angst; that is what I wished for. I especially didn't want history to repeat itself and for either of them to have to go through what I'd been through.

Dave and I would have dealt with it differently of course.

Mum still, after all these years couldn't talk openly. She listened to Charlotte and answered in monosyllables;

I should have realised that we would never achieve more than that, she simply wasn't capable of such open discussion, nor would she ever be.

Many weeks later, on one of her Sunday visits, we had eaten lunch and cleared away and had retired to the lounge. Mum suddenly blurted out that I had better have these (holding out two bits of paper) and promptly burst onto tears.

The two pieces of paper were a letter from my social worker and a photograph of Lena aged six months. I couldn't believe my eyes. Mum and Dad had kept them from me for twenty-eight years. Mum said it was Dad's decision to keep them from me to save me any further heartache. Seeing as he wasn't there to defend himself I had to take that with a pinch of salt. Did they never consider the effect of not talking about it had had on me?

The letter told me that Lena had settled well with her adoptive parents and was a happy well-adjusted little girl. It also told me that Lena had a brother who had also been adopted. The photo should have been something I'd have treasured for twenty-eight years but they had taken that away from me too.

I consoled mum and we talked of other things that afternoon.

Later when I was able to give it more clear concise thought, I was very bitter to think that they had kept those items from me. They had no right.

Even after I had talked to them four years earlier about how I was going to make any future decisions. Then was the time to release those pieces of paper. My dad had cried on that occasion, were they just crocodile tears? He had been dead for over two years, why had she waited until now? It just didn't add up. What use was a picture of a six-month-old baby who was now nearly thirty? She looked just like Emily and Charlotte at that age. I felt hurt and confused all over again.

*

That same summer '03 we had a great holiday with our friends from Gloucester. We hired a canal longboat and cruised 'The Cheshire Ring'. The eight of us got on so well together and in such a confined space remained dear friends right to the end of the week, and through the 102 locks.

That year the little boy I was working with moved to another school, which left me with only nine hours on my contract. I could have managed financially but felt I could be doing more so applied for a teaching assistant post at the local junior school.

Emily had been at that school and had recently moved to senior school and Charlie was still there and would be for another three years before also moving on to senior school.

I made sure Charlie didn't mind me working at *her school* and put in my application. The interview with the Head and the SENCO (Special Educational Needs Co-ordinator) went well, I was offered the job later that same day. I had worked at the school some three years previously as a dinner lady and knew my way round and it felt like coming home.

The boy I was to work with, I had worked with in his reception year at my previous school, so the fact that we knew each other was a bonus. We were able to build a working relationship from there; I looked forward to the challenge.

It was June when I had the interview and the job was due to start start in September.

During that summer break the four of us had a holiday in a hotel on the beach, this time in Menorca. We chose to go half-board this time so ended up supermarket shopping for snack items to have at lunchtime. We also had to buy litres and litres of bottled water for our daytime cuppas and soft drinks. We decided then that we had been better off having the all inclusive option, as on previous holidays.

We loved the island and did quite a bit of sightseeing and an awful lot more of lazing by the pool or on the beach. It was a very relaxing holiday. The girls made friends and we saw very little of them during the day on the days that we stayed at the hotel. From our hotel room we could walk up a few steps to the pools or down a few steps to the beach. We would usually touch base with the girls just before dinner each night.

CHAPTER EIGHTEEN

Towards the end of 2004 things started to get on top of me for some reason. I don't know what triggered it or what fuelled it but everything seemed to be a problem. I was tearful all the time and our relationship was suffering because of it.

I went to the doctor for a routine check up to discuss my thyroxine levels. I sat and poured my heart out to him.

My marriage was in tatters, my dad had died, I'd fallen out with my brother, and my adopted daughter *still* hadn't got in touch with me.

My marriage wasn't in tatters; it just was going through a rocky patch. My dad was dead but maybe I hadn't grieved as much as I should. I'd fallen out with my brother but there were two of us in this argument (not just me) and lastly Lena could not be influenced by anything I did, it was all beyond my 'control'. Everything seemed blacker than it was because I was so depressed.

I burst into floods of tears and said I couldn't cope any more. He looked at me aghast and said he had known me for twenty years and had never seen me upset before. The stupidest question I ever heard in my life came from his lips next, "Did I miss my adopted daughter?" I had a heartache that was bigger than my heart itself, of course I missed her!

He said he was going to refer me for some counselling and in the meantime to help in the short term he prescribed an anti-depressant drug.

I only took one of the tablets because I didn't like the way they made me feel. I was devoid of any emotion, happy or sad. I felt like a zombie.

The counselling appointment took a number of weeks to come through. In fact I had a letter asking me if I still required the appointment.

You would either have had a full blown nervous breakdown in that time or done as I had done and just bumbled along waiting for the appointment to come through. Eventually I had my first appointment with my lovely counsellor Catherine, she told me that I would see her once a fortnight for an hour at a time and I was entitled to six sessions.

We started to talk and the floodgates were opened, nothing was going to stop me talking about my story now.

Catherine was a very good listener and steered the conversation into all sorts of nooks and crannies and asked me to look inside them. I found our sessions to be the most therapeutic thing that had ever happened to me.

I was liberated, I had a voice and what I had to say was interesting. Catherine let me talk and talk and was so professional that the healing process was started straight away. Even after two sessions I was able to talk to Dave about Lena, the lock was undone.

After four sessions I started to talk seriously to Mum. She was never going to take on board what I was saying; she refused to accept any responsibility. Catherine had said to me that the sackcloth and ashes I'd been wearing for thirty years was not necessary because it was not all my fault and I should no longer beat myself up over it. She said that my parents were as much to blame for my pregnancy because they hadn't protected me sufficiently. She was totally amazed that they had thrown me out in the street to fend for myself; they should never have assumed I'd go to Dave's.

It was as if I needed permission to salve the guilt I'd carried for so long and Catherine was the one to do it. It was a totally refreshing experience and one that should have happened many years before.

I was more assertive without being too controlling (I hope). I was also asked a bit about my parents' child-hoods and it was suggested that they were the way they were due to outside influences in their lives. Some things would never be put completely right and my mother would remain one of those things.

After all the counselling sessions were done I tried to talk some more with Mum. Her bog standard response was that she couldn't understand why I had to bring it all up again. Again? It hadn't been talked about the first time so how could I be bringing it up again?

Mum had never in her life looked at anything from someone else's point of view, she just wasn't capable. It was the most frustrating part about my coming out of the wilderness and seeing things clearer than ever before.

She even implied that it had all been down to Dad and she was squeaky clean!

That made me really cross because he wasn't there to defend himself and she was besmirching his memory. She said that she had wanted to keep Lena and bring her up as her own but Dad wouldn't hear of it.

This was total nonsense (and a blatant lie) and just her way of clutching at straws. It was no use; we were flogging a dead horse. I was a teenager again trying to buck the system and not getting anywhere at all.

I had to try to get on with things as they were. I felt so differently in myself that I didn't want things left as they used to be at all. Some things you could never change.

I couldn't get her to admit that the counselling was useful and should have been done at the time of Lena's birth. If I wanted to apportion any blame to her I could just forget it.

*

The straw that finally broke the camels back happened some months later at Charlotte's ninth birthday party. It was traditional to celebrate with a barbecue for Charlotte's birthday because it is in May. All the rest of us have winter birthdays. It was a good excuse to get everyone together that had been at her Christening barbecue. It was usually the first barbecue of the season.

Since Dad's death Mum had come to us most Sundays. Because it was Charlie's birthday Monica and Mike, Jayne and Ray and Denise plus both mum's were invited. It was always a busy time getting ready for that many people and I was doing things in the kitchen. Mum was still driving at the time. We asked her if she would kindly pick Hilda up and bring her along. This was to save Dave fetching his mum who only lived two streets away from my mum.

When the two mums arrived together Hilda came into the kitchen first. I kissed her in welcome and got on with jobs. When my mum came into the kitchen I also kissed her in welcome and got back to what I was doing.

The day wore on, everyone was fed and watered and the meal was a huge success. The cake was brought out and we sang 'Happy Birthday'. The presents were opened and a jolly time was had by all.

I got the feeling that my mum was a bit icy in her responses to me. I thought that maybe I hadn't waited on her as much as I usually did and that she would soon get over it.

That same week I went over to visit mum as usual and her iciness hadn't thawed. I asked her straight away what the problem was, due to my newfound assertiveness. She said that I had said hello to Hilda before I'd said hello to her.

She was a seventy-six-year-old woman and she was sulking! I said that for one thing she was being silly and it just happened that Hilda had arrived in the house before she had. She replied that I'd always thought more of Hilda than of her and as that was the case she was writing me out of her will. How much more controlling did she think she could do?

I had had enough!

I said, "I really love you mum and if you wish to cut me out of your will that is entirely up to you. If you believe that all I've ever done for you was with that in mind you have a very dim view of me. I am very fond of Hilda and I think you have always been jealous of that fact. I feel I need to remind you yet again that it was you and Dad who threw me out on the street. Hilda took me in and was more of a mother than you ever were. I'm walking out of the house now before I say something I'm going to regret." I was shaking but I stayed calm and spoke from the heart.

I walked out of the house and got into my car and drove away at speed. I was absolutely furious. Who the hell did she think she was, treating me like a puppet on a string to be manipulated?

I was so scared of the anger inside me that I drove straight to Hilda's house and cried on her shoulder. After tea and sympathy I was calm enough to drive home. Never ever did Hilda criticise anything my parents had done in the past and on this occasion she didn't condemn my mum's actions. Hilda knew when to sit firmly on the fence.

For the next five weeks we had no contact at all, I played her at her own stupid game. Until that time she had been to me every Sunday since losing my dad. I had also been going over to her house and doing a bit of housework for her. She was finding it increasingly difficult to stand for any length of time and was often short of breath. Fifty years of smoking was taking its toll.

She would bloody well need me before I needed her that was for certain.

After the five weeks I knew that yet again I had to be the adult and make the first contact. My therapy sessions had made me more assertive and I knew mum wouldn't be the big man and make a move towards me. I turned up the next Sunday afternoon with a plated up roast dinner and a jug of gravy. Her iciness was still firmly in place and she was going to carry that bitterness to her grave.

Nothing I could do or say would heal the rift this time. Every time I tried to get her to see a bit of reason we would go back to square one. I was so exasperated I swore badly again and she told me to leave the house if I couldn't moderate my tongue. This I did, not returning until the following Sunday with an identical plate and jug.

Eventually I called a truce and said that we would have to agree to disagree. She wasn't capable of making an apology for the way I had been treated aged sixteen.

It was too long ago and she wanted to remain right even if she was wrong. She certainly wasn't going to tell me who I could greet and in what order in my own house.

I noticed when I visited that she was doing less and less about the house but I decided that I wouldn't offer to do anything in case she thought I was trying to get my inheritance back. I wanted her to ask me if I could do a little bit of housework for her. She seemed content to sit and smoke and watch the television. She never mentioned the conversation or threat of cutting me out of her will. If you don't talk about something it will be forgotten? That was always her head in the sand approach.

The weeks rolled by and she enlisted the help of my sister-in-law Karen. Mum rang her up and said, "When you go to Sainsbury's for your shopping could you get me a few bits please?" She would reel off a small shopping list and Karen would get the things and deliver them to mum on her way home.

When I called to see her she would give me a small shopping list and I would do the same. When the girls and I called it was not unheard of that she would say, "Nanny just needs to finish watching this programme, then we can talk." She was living for all the soaps as I'm sure a lot of old people do.

I wasn't happy about buying her cigarettes but didn't want to have another argument. It was a bit late in the day for her to be giving up smoking. Mum only came for Sunday lunch if Dave or I fetched her over. She had given up driving for some reason. She asked the two oldest grandsons to do a little bit of shopping or gardening too. Much later we worked out that she was spreading it all about so we didn't realise just how little she was doing herself.

*

The huge argument we'd had back in May was not forgotten but was far enough in the past to be less painful. The year was wearing on; by September I counted up and realised that mum hadn't left the house for six weeks. I tried to cajole her into driving over to me for dinner but it just wasn't going to happen.

She wrote the excuse book and was using every last one she knew. She even started to say that she didn't feel well enough to drive.

Her legs were becoming increasingly swollen and she sat for many hours in front of the box. As the month progressed the swelling got worse and became painful to the touch. The skin couldn't stretch any further and she seemed to be filling up with water. The doctor would call and prescribe different water tablets but nothing seemed to make any difference.

One day I called and she hadn't got dressed. It was quite alarming to think that she was becoming so infirm. I phoned Karen with my fears.

When my sister-in-law and I were having lengthy telephone conversations about Mum and about my recent counselling sessions I falsely believed she was reporting back to my estranged brother. I wanted him to understand a little bit of how I'd been treated and the person I was, the anorexia and everything else. I thought that by pouring out my heart to Karen I could get through to Paul.

Mum still said on many occasions that she wished we could make up. I discovered much, much later that Karen hadn't passed on to Paul about my soul searching. She knew that Paul was as stubborn as our father had been and would speak to me only if it was necessary.

Jayne by this time had moved to a bungalow in Tattershall to be near her beloved golf club at Woodhall Spa. She didn't see Mum as often as she did when she lived in Peterborough. Mum had been over to Jayne and Ray's new place only once when Paul and Karen had taken her over there for lunch.

CHAPTER NINETEEN

It was Thursday lunchtime and Karen phoned to say that Mum had gone into hospital. Karen worked in the district hospital and had been told that mother-in–law was in A&E and phoned me straight away.

It transpired that mum had got up that morning and decided she could stand the pain in her legs no longer. She had phoned for an ambulance and had admitted herself to hospital. Knowing her hatred of hospitals and the number of years she had wasted in them visiting Dad I should have known it was quite serious for mum to go out on a limb to do this. I remembered as well that she'd been very reluctant to go in the ambulance when Dad and I were blue light dashed to Leicester.

Charlotte and I went to the hospital as soon school finished and by this time mum was still in A&E. Mum said that she was really fed up with it and was determined to stay until they did something positive for her. The doctors had seen her and were making arrangements to get her onto a ward for the night.

When Charlie and I left at about nine o'clock mum was safely ensconced in her hospital bed and was eating the chocolates we had taken her. I was shocked to see what a struggle she had to get herself onto the bed. When we left we waved and she waved back and we said our usual, Love you and see you tomorrow.' She replied Love you too." We'd said that to each other readily but I'm not sure how heartfelt it was sometimes!

Today I really meant it because I hated leaving her in hospital. Selfishly I wondered, was I going to spend many weeks hospital visiting?

That was Thursday night; on Friday morning at 7am I had that most dreaded of phone calls to say that Mum had taken a turn for the worse and could my brother and sister and I get to the hospital as soon as possible. It was a complete shock.

Paul had already gone to work and would be some time turning round and coming back to Peterborough. Karen had phoned him but had tried for a while with no signal to Paul's phone.

Jayne had an hour and a half drive from her bungalow to the hospital. I asked Dave to phone her but when he spoke to her he didn't say it was vital she get there soon, only that Mum was slightly worse.

I was first to arrive and found Mum in a very sorry state. She was on oxygen and was slipping away fast. I think she knew I'd arrived and slipped even further away. One hour passed then two and I sat by her bedside talking quietly and reassuring her that I would stay with her. I held her hand.

Eventually I phoned Jayne on my mobile outside the hospital to see how much longer she expected to be before arriving. Jayne said she had done one or two jobs before getting on the road and had then hit a traffic jam and was detouring. She said she'd be about another forty minutes before being with us. I had to tell Jayne that Mum had already slipped into a coma and would most likely leave us today. What a shock when you're driving along! Jayne hadn't realised the severity of the situation.

I went back to see Mum and Paul had arrived. We fell into each others arms and he said to me simply, "I've missed you."

This was his apology and was as good as it was ever going to get. It didn't matter; we were talking again. I think even to this day if we ever did a post mortem on that argument, we'd still both be right.

Soon after Jayne arrived and the three of us were round the bedside, just as the four of us had been at Dad's bedside four years earlier. We were deeply shocked at how quickly things had moved on.

The nurses had moved Mum to a side ward during the early hours of the morning and it was now lunchtime. They came in periodically to make her comfortable when she slipped down on her pillows but that was all. They pretty much left us all alone.

When it got to teatime Paul insisted that Jayne and I get something to eat so we went back to my house and I sorted a meal out for the rest of my family and Jayne and myself.

As soon as we'd eaten we got straight back to the hospital and let Paul go home for his evening meal. By 7.30pm we were all three back on duty. Mum hadn't changed all day really. When I'd arrived at 7.30am there was a flicker but then she had slipped away. She never gained consciousness again.

By 10 o'clock we agreed that it was best to go home as things had remained unchanged for so many hours.

On the way out Paul asked the nurses to contact him first if there was any change in mums' condition. That was really nice of him and I went home and more or less straight to bed.

I offered Jayne a bed for the night but she said she wanted to get home too.

At two o'clock on Saturday the 1st October mum peacefully passed away. She had been in hospital for less than thirty-six hours. I'm quite convinced that she waited until she was on her own to die, unlike Dad who had waited until we were all with him.

The cause of death was smoking, her lungs had given up and her heart had stopped. Apparently the swelling was a good indication of heart failure, but I was unaware of that fact until later.

Paul let Jayne and I sleep until about six that morning and rang us both with the news.

We arranged to meet at Mums' house later that day to discuss what we had to do and how to go about it.

When we got to the house we found everything in 'apple pie' order. Why had mum got her 'house in order', did she know that her end was near?

We found the will and all her paper work. All three of us were executors and I was surprised to find that she hadn't changed her will at all. All those threats weeks previously about cutting me out of her will were just to make a point and to try to get her own way as usual.

As it was a Saturday there was nothing we could do until Monday on the legal side of things. Our first appointment was with the hospital bereavement officer who would tell us whom to see next and so on.

We then set about going through Mum's address book and ringing everyone that we knew to tell them that she had died. It was a most upsetting time to realise the finality of it all. The house would have to be cleared and sold and there was an awful lot of stuff there, mum had always been a hoarder!

It was mainly family phone numbers in the address book because Mum hadn't accumulated many friends in her lifetime. There was only one friend that I had to ring and she was an acquaintance through a kidney patient that Dad had befriended. Everything had revolved around Dad's illness.

Mum's sister-in-law Iris, whom Mum had fallen out with after Maurice died said, "I never knew a more wicked and nasty woman than your mother, she was always interfering somewhere, I jolly well won't be coming to the funeral!"

This was a particularly unkind thing to say when I was in the early stages of grief, but it was a sentiment quite a few people shared.

It was one thing for me to say horrible things about my own mother on occasion and for her to agree with them but to say hurtful things about her first was totally out of order.

I said, "Well I thought I'd better let you know." I signed off as soon as possible.

We were a bit worried that the house might be burgled so we agreed that we would follow Mum's will to the letter and take away the things she wanted us to have individually. Paul then called in and checked over the house in the coming weeks and months that everything was OK.

On the Monday morning we started the legal processes and saw the bereavement officer at the hospital who released mum's personal belongings and the death certificate to us.

An appointment with the registrar was next where we registered Mum's death.

Paul and I did this together as we didn't see the need for Jayne to come to Peterborough until the appointment with the funeral director.

It was a surreal situation and Paul and I spoke freely to each other as if nothing had ever been strained between us. You would have thought that we'd vie for leader position, Paul being number one son and I being the eldest but this wasn't the case because we were very conscious of each others feelings. Actually we were treading on eggshells!

We all went to see the same solicitor we had used after Dad died. He had been very professional in his manner and had put Mum at ease when she had to get probate granted.

Now we were going through the same procedure to get probate on Mum's estate to share three ways. I was still surprised that she hadn't made a codicil to her will cutting me out but she either hadn't meant the threat or she just hadn't got around to it.

Jayne and I could talk about anything and shared our spiritual beliefs. Jayne thought that when a person first dies they can be something else before they go to where they're going. Two days after Mum died, Jayne had a strange experience; she was gardening when a dragonfly landed on her hand. She blew on it to make it take off but it flew round and landed back on her shoulder. Jayne said out loud, "If that's you Mum, you can land on my hand again." The dragonfly landed back on her hand!

Charlotte had overheard me retelling this story to Dave. The next morning when I went in to wake her for school she said, "Nanny isn't a dragonfly any more, she's a bullfrog now."

What a strange thing to say. She knew that dragonflies only lived one day but where she got the idea of a bullfrog I will never know. Even more bizarre was the fact that Dave and I had sat on the patio the previous evening and had commented on a noisy frog in our pond. I want to believe that it was Mum finally saying, "Sorry."

I had ignored her because I didn't know she was a frog until Charlie told me the next day. It's a very romantic notion but it helps me.

We went to see the funeral director and arranged all the details there. Paul decided to use the rugby club for a small get together afterwards and this was also booked.

Jayne and I set about clearing the house of some of the stuff to keep busy before the funeral. With hindsight we could have taken our time to clear the place but it was our way of dealing with our loss.

We'd already taken the things she had willed to us individually. The dining furniture was Paul's now and arrangements were made to collect them and get them to his house.

*

I had a major guilt trip about going to the chapel of rest to see Mum. I had been on numerous occasions to sit and talk with Dad but I didn't feel I wanted to go and see Mum. I couldn't explain why but I didn't want to go.

I had taken the week off work as compassionate leave and had been at the house sorting and clearing as much as possible. I would fill my little car up to the roof with stuff for the charity shop and for every car full that I took there I took a car full to the tip. The amount of stuff you can collect in a lifetime is amazing!

On the fourth day, for some reason, before going to the house I stopped off at the chapel of rest. It had to be now or never, the funeral was fast approaching. I took a deep breath and ventured inside. The young man who came to see me was very kind and asked me to wait for two minutes while he got Mum ready. Another deep breath and in I went. Now I knew why I shouldn't have gone. Whereas Dad had looked so peaceful, Mum being a large lady had sunk into herself somehow and looked grotesque. I kissed her forehead and stroked her hands and left pretty hastily. I left the building and got into my car, it was a two-minute car journey to Mum's house. Halfway there I was conscious of a terrible noise in the car with me. It was me, I was keening.

I had gone into shock; when I got to the house I ran from room to room screaming. I was having a major panic attack and hyperventilating. I started to feel very faint and quickly rang Karen to come to help me. She had to make a mercy dash from her house to Mum's and knew by my breathing what had happened.

She calmed me down and the danger passed. She banned me from any more house clearance until after the funeral. I had been like a whirling dervish, and had over done things as usual.

*

The local vicar came to my house to talk about the service at the crematorium and Paul and Karen came over too. This was the first time back in my house for over five years for them.

After the vicar left we shared a bottle of red wine and promised to get together more often in the future.

We never did unpick that argument because we both believed we were right, it was best left unspoken.

The day of the funeral arrived. This would be the first one that our girls had attended. Everything ran as smoothly as expected. My greatest fear was that I would have another attack but that didn't happen either. After the service at the crematorium we all arrived at the rugby club and started to relax and chat with family.

Karen had bought Jayne and I a beautiful dragonfly broach each. How thoughtful of her, it is something to treasure forever. Jayne and I ended up drinking ourselves comatose and had to be taken home to sleep it off. I think we saw Mum off in a party atmosphere.

Grief is a very strange thing; it just creeps up and washes over you. I thought I was dealing with it quite well and letting tears flow unchecked when the need arose. One evening about a week after the funeral I was getting the evening meal ready when I started to cry. It was like a big fat chewy bit of grief that had to be dealt with. It was unadulterated raw emotion.

Dave said, "Come on, stop that crying now, all you ever did when your Mum was alive was to fight with her. You were always moaning about her and calling her names so I think that's enough tears don't you?"

I couldn't believe what I was hearing, I thought Dave of all people understood how I felt inside and the hang-ups' I had. She was still my mother and even though we hadn't always seen eye to eye, I loved her unconditionally.

Catherine had warned me right at the beginning of the year that I would never get Mum to admit to any blame on her and Dad's part but I'd still had to try. That was what we had argued about most severely and I would have to live with the fact that Mum had died and

I hadn't been able to say I was sorry. There I was still carrying the guilt for things that couldn't be altered.

There was so much to sort out with the house sale and utility bills and finances. It was a mammoth task. The solicitor took the bulk of the paperwork and dealt with it directly for us.

At one time I thought it would be a good investment for Dave and I to buy out Paul and Jayne's share of the house. I had an idea that we could modernise it and let it out. We even went to a financial advisor to sort out a buy to let mortgage. The only problem was the purchase price, which Paul didn't agree on. I was willing to pay the asking price He didn't want to see me make a huge profit in years to come. We ended up selling the house on the open market. Looking back it probably wouldn't have worked anyway. I was too emotionally involved with the property.

As it turned out we were nearly twelve months before the house was sold and the estate finalised.

Even though we'd cleared the house so rapidly we still had to maintain it for all of those months afterwards.

The saddest things we found were thirty years worth of diaries. They were not the sort of dairies that gushed feelings, they were more factual. They had entries like 'went to Sainsbury's then called in to see Helen and the girls.'

They catalogued dates of deaths and births or operations and things like that, daily humdrum life.

It was probably a mistake to read them but they were irresistible.

The entry for the 16th July 1974 said 'Helen weds today.' I wanted it to say something like, 'My darling daughter gets married today. Even though we won't be sharing her day with her I hope she'll always be happy. I wish we hadn't been so stubborn and had gone to the wedding.' Ha ha, some hope!

The entry for the 9th March 2001 said 'Ken died.' I wanted something like, 'My life ended today. My dearest husband and soul mate has left me. My heart is broken.'

Her last weeks were more painful than any of us had realised when she wrote, 'Feel really bad today. Legs no better.'

Of our final argument she wrote, 'Helen thinks more of Hilda than me, always has done. That bloody German.'

So here I was aged 47 with both parents gone and still no sign that Lena was wondering about me. It had taken a long time to 'grow up' properly. The one thing to come out of it all was that I was no longer angry inside, I was a lot calmer. I had learned to be more assertive without the anger. I was so incredibly sad inside but as always had to trudge on.

I still carried guilt that Mum and I had argued and not made up properly before she died. The thing was I had spent an awful lot of years being good. I had to focus on that fact, it was too late to worry about how she had felt about me in her final weeks.

One more distressing thing to happen was that Paul and Jayne fell out. It was almost as if Paul could only cope with one sister at a time! He'd fallen out with me when Dad died, now he'd fallen out with Jayne on Mum's death.

He and I were on talking terms again and now the twins were at loggerheads. It was when the probate was taking so long to go through. This was the solicitors' fault. Jayne had phoned Paul to see what could be done to speed up things and Paul said, "All you've ever wanted was to get your hands on the money." Jayne was so incensed that she hung up on him. Typical of our family that at the first sign of trouble a falling out would occur and months or years of silence would follow.

CHAPTER TWENTY

When all the money from the sale of the house and the shares and investments came through Dave and I were in a strong financial position. We enlisted the help of an independent financial adviser and hopefully invested my inheritance wisely. We also looked at the possibility of moving house again. We looked at a couple of properties but found them lacking in one area or another. We'd been told it would cost about fourteen thousand pounds to finance a move. Stamp duty, solicitors and estate agents fees. We decided to stay where we were but to have a loft conversion.

The project was to last three months and we would gain a large new master bedroom and en-suite bathroom.

Our property would be transformed into a four-bedroom, two-bathroom one. The cost would be around eighteen thousand pounds.

This seemed a good investment and we would see what we were getting for our money. A house move would use up a lot of money on unseen costs. The reality of the conversion was that it took a whole year of stress before completion.

The first appointment with the architect was on the 6th April 2006. We saw the last tradesman, the plasterer on the 15th May 2007. Dave was then free to get on with the decorating.

The year in between was so stressful it's a wonder we survived. I kept a diary of events in case the whole thing went horribly wrong and there was any legal wrangling. I only really did that because Peter and Jenny had experienced a bad builder, down in Torquay, and had gone to court in the end. I hoped that wouldn't happen to us but wrote everything down just in case.

*

Dave had celebrated his fiftieth birthday back in February and we'd had one of my famous parties.

We also booked a 'big' holiday. In the August of 2006 it was a blessed relief to get away from the building site for a fortnight by the pool and the sea. The builder was in the process of moving a wall and fitting a new family bathroom. The loft conversion was still at the planning stage. That part of the project didn't actually start until January of 2007.

As it was Dave's holiday to celebrate his half-century he chose to go back to Menorca. We went to a different resort and went all-inclusive again. It was our most expensive holiday to date because it was no longer appropriate to have a family room. We had one room for us and one room for the girls.

Also Emily's fare was at the adult rate as she had turned fourteen. The hotel was right on the beach just how we like it and the pool was fantastic. It was a very lazy holiday and most enjoyable. The girls made lots of friends as usual and they would range around the hotel in groups. The best thing about being all-inclusive was that the girls could get refreshments whenever they wanted.

All in all life was pretty good. We were settled and happy and that goes a long long way.

Just one final push to get this loft conversion done and then maybe we could relax. It really was the most stressful time because the builder didn't communicate very well. He knew what was happening but didn't appreciate that we also needed to know. He would tell us that things were going to happen on a particular day and then when the day arrived, he didn't!

At one point I threatened him with eviction from the site. I said I'd get another builder in to finish the job. I'm sure he knew that was unlikely as where would I get a reliable builder to finish the job, it would have delayed the project even more.

We went away on our usual Norfolk retreat at Easter hoping that when we got back we could see the job almost completed. That didn't happen either and we had another month of stress before it was finally finished.

It is a fantastic addition to our already lovely home and we are absolutely thrilled with the finished product.

The only thing that could happen now to make my life complete and totally fulfilled would be for Lena to get in touch. I hoped and prayed that it wouldn't be too many years more before we'd be reunited.

*

The summer of 2007 we had a really lovely holiday with our friends from Gloucester again. We went out to Dave's old company villa again. Originally there were going to be six of us, we were leaving our older teenagers at home (Emily 15 and Zoe 17.)

During May of the same year Emily discovered alcohol. We were over at my nieces' home for dinner and had intended to stay over in Spalding to save either of us driving. Only half an hour into the evening I received a phone call from the police asking if I was the parent of Emily Hudson.

She had been with friends in town and they had somehow got hold of vodka. She had passed out and her friends had called an ambulance. The police officer informed me that as she was a minor we would have to be present. They were taking her to Peterborough District Hospital and we were to rendezvous there. Dave and I made the dash from Spalding to Peterborough in about twenty minutes (nearly having to stop three times for me to be physically sick with the worry of what we were going to find.) We discovered that the police had released Emily and her boyfriend to his mother's house. We changed tack and drove over there and picked Emily up and brought her home to sober up. My first question was, Do we need to get you the morning after pill?" Emily sluringly said, "No, she hadn't had sex." Why was it that she had such little respect for us?

The next day she was very shocked at the gaps in her memory and quite remorseful. My mind was made up, I couldn't trust her to be left on her own so she was forced to come to Spain with us and swelled our number to seven people. Karen and Nigel drove all the way from Peterborough to Castillons Vida over a two-day period. Holly, Emily, Dave and myself flew out to Spain. We had a very relaxing ten days together and again remained good friends throughout. As there were seven of us we adopted the names of the seven dwarves and stayed in role the whole holiday. Dave-Grumpy, Nigel-Doc,

Karen-Sleepy, Emily-Bashful, Charlie-Dopey, Holly-Sneezy and me being Happy!! Great fun, we all had a fantastic time.

Since Emily was only thirteen years old she has been a very moody and isolated teenager. She spent endless hours in her bedroom emerging only to 'graze'.

She has discovered, as all teenagers do, that their parents are crap and are not to be respected in the slightest. I especially, received the major brunt of her displeasure because I am around more than Dave. Emily and I fought all the time and Dave often came home from work to a very fraught atmosphere.

He finds it very difficult to back me at all and will often sigh and say, "Just leave it will you Helen." Anything for a quiet life!

If I am nagging about a particular issue this results in Emily finding the crack in our armour and fighting even more valiantly the next time. She has made a huge wedge in our relationship, resulting in me threatening to leave on more than one occasion. It is no good now even thinking about a clip round the ear, as we used to get, she has hit me back several times; she can put up a good fight and no one is the winner.

Charlotte on the other hand sees the bad behaviour displayed by Emily and mimics it. She also is at a very selfish stage and thinks the whole world revolves around her. She slams doors and shouts and screams and generally makes my life pretty miserable. When things reach a crescendo and she sees how upset I am she will go away and think about things and then apologise. This is soon forgotten though and the same thing will occur very rapidly. At least Charlotte tries hard to make our relationship work but this only makes Emily more jealous, referring to her as 'Golden Girl'.

Emily thought she could bunk off school earlier this year when fear got the better of her. She should have been sitting her French oral exam (GCSE) that day but decided to feign sickness. I allowed her to stay at home confident that she'd never 'swung the lead' before.

A phone call from her school mid morning put me right and the exam had to be rescheduled. I was absolutely furious with her.

I'd love to be able to analyse where I went wrong with my errant teenagers.

When I talk to parents with similar aged children I always feel assured that they are going through much the same thing but it doesn't make it any easier. I seem to have spent my whole life fighting my parents only to lose them and then start fighting my children.

*

Earlier this year I celebrated my fiftieth birthday with yet another wonderful party. My fantastic husband took me to Paris for a few days in February. My dearest friend from Gloucester came to look after the house and the girls so that we didn't have to worry about anything while we were away. It was a lovely holiday and the first in many years with just the two of us. I absolutely adored the city and would love to go back in the future.

I've calculated that Lena's adoptive parents will probably be in their sixties now and sadly I have to wait for one or both of them to die. Even then there are no guarantees that she will contact me. I just hope that she will.

*

The summer of 2008 the four of us went back to Dave's old company villa yet again. I romantically thought that it would be the very last time that the four of us would ever go on holiday as a family unit again. What a nightmare it was. Emily made it very plain that she didn't want to go but I booked it anyway. The previous year she had been forced to come with us and had quite enjoyed the days by the pool. I hoped that when she got there she would be OK. I reassured her that it really was the last time that she would have to put up with us and to grin and bear it for two short weeks.

She absolutely ruined it with her behaviour leading up to the holiday and during the two weeks of our stay.

It didn't matter to her that there were three other people whose holiday it was, she was going to spoil it anyway, and she did. Her selfish attitude started months before as she would use the 'cracked record' approach, constantly repeating that she didn't want to go. I would assume the same 'cracked record' and say simply, "You have to go, we can't leave you at home." This went on backwards and forwards constantly until we both gave up and didn't speak about it at all.

I actually believe that more than half of the pleasure of a holiday is the 'looking forward to it' part. That was taken away from me as every time I said something like, "Won't it be great by the pool?" She would say, "Will you stop talking about the crappy holiday!" I reminded her that it was Dads, Charlie's and my 'crappy' holiday as well. This made not a scrap of difference, she was hell bent on ruining it.

Emily knows all the right buttons to push to get me in a state and constantly does it.

When disciplining Charlie for something out of order Emily would tell me constantly what a bad parent I was and try to increase the amount or severity of the punishment. Always bemoaning the fact that I'm harder on her, which is totally unfounded of course. Jealousy again. I've told Emily on numerous occasions that there is no need to be jealous, as we love both girls equally. I've also said that I don't want another Charlotte, or Golden Girl, as she puts it, but just an Emily who has respect for me in particular.

Dave will do absolutely anything for a quiet life and would rather leave any disciplining to me but will endlessly say, "Just leave it love."

Both girls know that we don't show a united front and chip away at the veneer all the time.

I feel as if the three of them are ganging up on me to make me feel miserable. They seem to take it in turns to have a go at me about something or other.

We met another family on holiday in Spain with similar aged teenagers and I found myself talking to Paula (the mum) about how depressed I was feeling because of my lot.

It was encouraging to discover that she was experiencing the same sort of problems and the same feelings as me. The Yates family helped me to keep my sanity whilst away in Spain, I don't think I could have done it without them.

Years ticking by, still hoping Lena will come to find me, still hoping to hold the family together, still hoping to stay sane and sometimes happy.

CHAPTER TWENTY-ONE

The 16th October 2008 was an auspicious date. I was talking to Charlotte whilst opening the mail. The letter I received stopped my chatter in mid flow.

I was informed by The General Register Office that the law had changed and I would be able to register with them as a birth mother. Lena could be traced! There was one small proviso, if the adoptee didn't want any contact then that would be the end of the matter. If Lena agreed to contact, a mediator would be put in place to ensure that counselling was available every step of the way towards a reunion.

On the 21st October I found a few peaceful minutes to go onto the Internet to download the required form. I soon filled out the details, wrote a cheque for £30, added Lena's birth certificate and my marriage certificate. I sealed the envelope and walked shakily to the post box. On the short walk to the letterbox I sent up a silent prayer that things would finally be on their way towards some closure. With a gentle kiss of the envelope I dropped the letter into the box.

I walked home full of hope and anticipation.

I admitted to Jayne the next day on the phone that I was really scared for all the upset and angst I could foresee. Now I must just do as I've done for the last 34 years; wait and see.

By early in November I received a letter from The General Register Office telling me that I was already registered and returned my cheque for £30. When I had a little delve in my folder I discovered that I had indeed registered in February '97. They were called The National Statistics Register then. The General Register Office told me that as soon as Lena filled in her half of the form a match would be made. I knew all of this from all those years ago so what about this change in the law?

I was on my own that afternoon and carried on with my housework feeling like I'd been kicked in the stomach. The grief came up from my toes and I sobbed and sobbed. I was completely beside myself but actually did allow the indulgence of grief to wash over me.

When Dave got home later he knew something was seriously wrong. We were able to talk and he got it in perspective for me. In reality, I was in no different a position than

before the letter arrived. I just had to get on with waiting again. This I felt was something I really was good at.

My relationship with Emily was no better and the total disrespect she showed me just got worse. The main problem was that whenever I had to nag her about any aspect of her behaviour, Dave would undermine me. As always my man would do anything for a quiet life so when I was bad cop he always played good cop.

In November 2009 Emily started a Saturday job at Somerfield supermarket. It was good that she could earn a little bit and was lucky enough to use my car. The problems started after Christmas, we would often get a phone call to say that Emily was due into work. These were extra shifts during the Christmas holidays. She was often asleep and when woken refused point blank to move herself and get there a little late. She would blame their poor rota administration, it was never her. After several phone calls I could see where this was going to lead. At the end of January she came home and told me she had lost her job. I stupidly rang the manager in a rage and told him that he couldn't just do that and that there were procedures that had to be followed. He was able to calmly tell me that he had given Emily the required number of verbal warnings and so was well within his rights to sack her. She as usual CBA (couldn't be arsed) but I was mortified, my generation were embarrassed, there was huge stigma attached. Of course that little interlude would not appear on the C.V.

In June '10 Emily and long-standing boyfriend, Josh leave school. Without a job between them they could have as much "duvet time" as they liked. Emily was due to start college in September, her course was computer maintenance. Josh was going to Swansea University in October to study engineering. The whole summer stretched ahead of them and I was totally fed up with the amount of time they spent here and the amount of meals I was providing, while all they did was play computer games, most days Emily didn't even get dressed. I resigned myself that it wouldn't be for much longer until Josh went to Swansea. As it turned out it was not meant to be. This very intelligent boy who had everything going for him decided that it was not for him. His parents hired a large car to transport him and all his creature comforts to Swansea on a Sunday afternoon. Even before they were back in Peterborough Josh had phoned Emily to say he hated it and was coming home! When Ems told me this I was amazed and said to her, "tell him not to be so silly, he only has to get through fresher's fortnight and then he'll be home!" I couldn't believe it. By Tuesday evening he was home and so basically had spent only hours in Swansea. If I'd been his mother I'd have superglued him to that bed and made him persevere. He only had to endure the first year in halls as the following two years he could lodge with family. He would have been able to come home every weekend on the train as his father works for the railway. His Grandmother had already said she would cover all his fees so he would be debt free.

So here was the situation, nothing had changed so I decided to talk to them both. I explained that some changes had to be made and that they would have to spend a little more time at Josh's house. I think they were both shocked that I was rocking their boat.

In November 2010 Ems got a job in IT. She'd done some work experience with James at P C Solve and he was now able to offer her a part-time job. She was in college three days and worked for James the other three days. James is married to a teacher friend of mine called Isabel and it was through me that Ems got the job. James is a very enterprising guy, he has managed to build his business from just him working from home doing PC repairs to letting an industrial unit and two shops, employing twelve people. He no longer has the unit but has the two shops, one in Peterborough and one in Spalding.

Now that Ems was earning I thought it was high time she should pay some board and lodgings. I thought £20 a week was a fair price, Ems on the other hand didn't agree at all. She seemed to think that it was her home and her right to live there. After heated debate that was obviously going nowhere I decided that the only way to get through to her was via a Power Point. I called it "The facts of life" and in it I listed all the outgoing costs to running a big house like ours. I calculated that actually £80 per week was a more realistic figure. The upshot of it all was that she had to pay up and look good, she finally realised that she was on a very good deal. The main problem was that she didn't appreciate that legally we didn't have to put a roof over her head as she was 17 years old. In the future I would be pushed to my absolute limit with her attitude and generally bad behaviour.

CHAPTER TWENTY-TWO

Around this time Hilda was diagnosed with dementia. When she first told us we didn't believe it at all. As time went on we had to accept that it really was happening. I was more than happy to have her to Sunday lunch every other week. I was loathe to let it be every Sunday as I had with my own Mother because I knew how hard it was on the rest of the family and the restrictions it placed on doing family stuff or even going away. In the beginning she would forget simple words like television and we had to try to guess what she was telling us about. Soon every sentence that she tried to put together was missing at least one word as she forgot the names of the most fundamental things. As my work schedule allowed me to visit her often I started to do so. Her Doctor contacted me with a view to getting Hilda on a research programme. It required huge commitment on both our parts as I readily agreed to become Mum's main carer. We went ahead with the programme and the reward for it was six months on the dementia drug, which normally wasn't prescribed in these early stages. As in everything Hilda did during her life she did it with dignity and determination.

After some months it became clear to me that we needed some care in place as a lot of things were becoming difficult for Hilda to do. I got a care package in place and a social worker on board. Mum now had morning and evening care and I went over most afternoons to do bits and bobs and to cook an evening meal. Soon I had to increase the care to lunchtime as well and get meals on wheels as well. I started to realise that soon we would need to move her from her sheltered housing. We started to look at accommodation with 24/7 care with still some independent living. As it turned out waiting for a place to become available was a bridge too far. The morning carer rang me to say that she'd found Hilda on the floor and could I get there as soon as possible, she'd called an ambulance. I dashed over and arrived at the same time as the ambulance. It transpired that Mum had a nasty urine infection, which made her even more confused than normal. She'd somehow fallen out of bed and had laid on the floor most of the night. She was hospitalised and spent two weeks in hospital. When she came home, although catheterised, and needing an even more extensive care package she was still in her own home.

We carried on much as before but I was very aware that she was deteriorating and this move to the care home needed to happen sooner rather than later. In the end it didn't happen that way at all. Mum got another urine infection and ended up in hospital again. This time we had the added problem of a bed sore. Eventually with meetings with the social worker it was sadly decided to move Mum to a Nursing home. I had a look around one or two and was quite shocked at what I saw. I decided to opt for the same one that my Uncle Jimmy had been in for ten years and my cousin Steve (his son) had worked at. I couldn't have been more wrong, they placed Mum on the wing where the patients with dementia were far more advanced in their disease. Charlotte and I followed the ambulance from the hospital to the nursing home and tried to settle her in. We hated leaving her there when the time came and both burst into tears when we got in the car. It was like a hellhole with walking dead in it. There were screamers too. Some of the poor souls were so disorientated and frightened. The next day Dave and I went to Mum's bungalow and packed up a few pictures and favourite ornaments to try and make her room more "homely". When we got to the nursing home they had moved her to a wing with patients at a similar stage to Hilda. It was better but still not right and eventually I was able to move Mum to another much nicer home. The bedsore was still a major problem and eventually Mum was bedridden. The last twelve months were an absolute nightmare for us all, seeing the darling woman we all loved so dearly shrivel to a little old bag of bones, being fed puréed food. She was catheterised and was given regular enemas. There was nothing she could do for herself; she often said that she wanted to die.

The whole transition from Mum being in her own home to being in such a sorry state, I can honestly say that I did everything in my power to make her as comfortable as possible. I spent as many afternoons with her as I could and towards the end would drive home in tears as I knew we were losing her day-by-day.

One happy occasion was when Mark and Lizzie got married. Mark is Ronnie's son. It was like a military operation but I was determined that Hilda would see her grandson married. The wedding was at one o'clock and my operation started at ten when Dave and I went over to the nursing home to help the staff get Mum dressed. After this was achieved we put her in the car and drove to the hairdressers. From the car to the wheelchair and into the hairdressers. We left her there and dashed home for a late brunch and showers and getting ourselves ready. Next came the pick up from the hairdressers. Us four were being driven to the church by Josh and then he was coming back to the reception. Denise and Tom were in her car and it was arranged to meet at the hairdressers and all work together on installing Nanny in Denise's car. This was a lot harder than any of us realised as Mum was just a dead weight and not able to help in any way. The church was at Great Gidding and it was a perfect sunny day. When we did get into church Mum's wheelchair was pushed right to the front in pride of place but bless her she didn't really know what was going on. At one point Hilda whispered to me, "Who is that in the white dress?" Next was a little stroll to Lizzie's Aunty's house for photographs and bubbles and nibbles. As with all weddings this took a long while and I was quite concerned at the amount of time Hilda had been either in a car or in the wheelchair. At three o'clock we finally put Mum back in Denise's car and she was taken back to the nursing home and all the other guests went to the reception at the Sibson Inn.

At least she was on the photos and had a record of her lovely day. I knew for certain that that was going to be the last outing, and it was. Hilda was returned to her bed and due to all the handling she'd received those bedsores never cleared up. She was turned two-hourly day and night, her poor old body would never recover. On New Years Day 2013 I got that dreaded phone call. Hilda was very poorly and would we come straight away. When we arrived I knew that it would not be long and so spent a few minutes ringing the rest of the family.

Peter and Jenny were in Devon and had twice weekly
phone chats so it was natural to put my mobile to Mum's
ear and let them speak. She wasn't able to respond but it
helped them to be able to say goodbye. Next I phoned
Margaret and explained the situation. She was reluctant
to come as she had only just got back from being in the
area visiting someone else and had a long drive back to
Mum. She did come over later that same evening and sit
with Hilda and Denise was there too.

Before all the others arrived and after the very
emotional phone call with Peter and Jenny we just
sat and held her hands. I didn't want to leave her but
after some hours Dave said we must leave as there was
nothing we could do and that she may linger for many
more hours. I went out of the room and let Dave say his
goodbyes and then he went to the car park instructing
me to follow. It was then my turn to say farewell to this
wonderful woman who had been more of a mother than
my own mother had been. I sat and told her how much
I loved her and thanked her for everything she had done
for me. I could not leave and Dave had to ring me three
times to say, "Come now!"

I eventually had to do as Dave was asking me but it
was the biggest wrench. Other family came and sat and
eventually they had to go home. I got the phone call to
say Hilda had passed away at 8.30 am on the 2nd of
January.

Dave and I went back to the nursing home later that
day and I selected her wedding outfit for her to go to the
undertakers. We had another chance to say goodbye.
Now all the arrangements had to be made. The funeral
was the 16th January and if I say so myself we gave her
a fantastic send off. Her sister and brother in law came

over and stayed with us, even though Uncle Herbie was 85 and not in the best of health himself. They loved staying with us and we arranged a trip to Germany in the summer to visit them and also show the girls where Nanny had lived and played as a little girl.

Sadly after several different problems between Emily and myself she cried off and didn't join us on that holiday. Charlotte loved the trip and all the new experiences. We travelled up into the Harz Mountains and sprinkled mum's ashes at the back of her childhood home, over looking a lake in a beautiful wooded area. We finally had closure and it felt good.

CHAPTER TWENTY-THREE

During the previous twelve months and pretty much during the preceding seven years my relationship with Emily had deteriorated. So much so that in desperation I rang a works helpline. I was given five session of counselling with a wonderful woman called Mary Henchy. When I told my story from the beginning, because I'd told it so many times in the past I was able to stay dry-eyed. Not that that was an option. If I ever allowed myself to cry I might not be able to stop. When I finished and looked over at Mary, the tears were coursing down her face, the tissue box on my side had to be offered back to her. I was really shocked when she went on to call my parents f***ing b*****ds!

No one in all the 39 years had ever said that they had to admit to dealing with the situation badly. Of course they never had and had died with it. What I never forgave them for was holding back the letter and photo even when I asked them to let me be in control.

The next session we concentrated on my relationship with Emily. I had always, like any mother, blamed myself and assumed that my controlling nature was at fault. Emily had always been Lena and Emily rolled into one as far as I was concerned. I didn't want to lose another daughter but I had really about seven years previously when she became that truculent teenager. Now aged 21, it was about time that she realised just what a good deal she was on. Board and lodgings cheep as chips and the use of my car. Anyway, Mary's quip this time was, "The little t**t, it's about time she grew up!" Again I was shocked and encouraged that the fault was not all at my door.

Subsequent sessions were very enlightening and down the months I have tried to divorce myself from her and have as little contact as possible. One of the main problems has been Dave's inability to back me and when I play bad cop he thinks it's time to play good cop. It all culminated with a particularly bad argument about house rules when I threw Emily out. Bearing in mind she would be safe and go to Josh's, unlike myself all those years ago. She said, "Dad won't back you" and laughed in my face. Sure enough, when Dave came home he didn't back me and allowed her to stay.

The situation was so bad that just before we went to Germany, some very hurtful things were said by Emily, including the fact that she thought my house rules were no better than the Nazis disciplines during the war. I was so upset that I didn't contact her once during our time away. It hurt me to do so but she had to know how upset I was. Since our return things have been frosty to say the least. I really need her to move out.

CHAPTER TWENTY-FOUR

In May of '13 I received a letter telling me that I was eligible for mediation services through Northampton County Council and I set up a meeting in Kettering, which is half-way between Northampton and Peterborough. It appeared that after all my letter writing, down the years I had come to the top of the pile, so to speak. Oh my God, it was finally going to happen. What I didn't know. The day of the meeting approached and thankfully Charlie came with me for moral support. We met with a lovely lady called Frances Harvey and a colleague of hers called Margaret and we spent a good hour chatting. Firstly, I pretty much retold my story yet again and explained that not only would Lena find a birth mother but a biological father and two full sisters as well. Frances and Margaret listened patiently and then were able to explain the process that we would all go through. They explained it was a lengthy process and I said I'd already waited 39 years, what were a few more months if that was what it was going to be. The first step would be to make enquiries to find out if Lena was registered with a doctor in this country and this would establish the fact that she was alive. I'd always feared that maybe as a little girl she'd run out in the road and been run over and there was me waiting and grieving but not knowing. This next step was going to be a huge hurdle for me. We all agreed to move forward slowly and carefully with any amount of counselling along the way. Wasn't it bizarre that 39 years previously I got absolutely nothing! We exchanged email addresses and Frances said she was always on the end of a phone.

After a couple of weeks there was an email from Frances asking me to ring her. When I did it was amazing news, Lena was registered to a doctor in this country. All my fears about her dying were unfounded and we could move forward tentatively.

Frances would go ahead with a search. At our meeting in Kettering it was intimated that it was possible that she was no longer called Lena. I felt sad about that but what is in a name huh. Frances emailed again and again we spoke at length on the phone, she had found two possible matches, both with first name, second name and date of birth correct. Now I knew Lena's name was completely different but didn't ask what it was as I had a feeling that Frances wouldn't divulge it that at this stage. The next question was when I would like the letters to go out. It was a couple of weeks before our holiday in Germany and yet again Emily was being very tricky. I think as a knee jerk reaction I said could we wait until after our holiday. I still needed closure on my dear mother-in-law and this I hoped would happen when we sprinkled the ashes. Also with Emily being difficult I thought it could complicate any future meetings and to be very honest with myself, I was petrified in case we couldn't get it right. There was another huge hurdle, of course and that was if Lena didn't want any contact, for what ever reason then that would be the end of the matter. Frances, as usual was able to reassure me that these were all perfectly normal feelings but that it was also wise to wait until after the holiday. How awful would it be if contact could be made and then Frances would have to say to Lena "Your Mum is out of the country for two weeks so we have to wait!" So on the 12th August 2013 these two letters were sent out. Please God, one must be Lena and her own life is not too complicated and she wants contact.

*

In September '13 things really came to a head with Emily and yet again I felt forced to throw her out. On this occasion Dave did back me and said that she would have to go. She stood her ground and refused to go, so we were in a stalemate situation. The awful situation forced me to take her off my car insurance and let her make her own way to work. This of course she achieved by getting Josh to take her into Spalding. I was shocked at how upset Dave was over the whole affair and saw him age by ten years in front of me. I then decided that some talking was in order and texted Emily to suggest a truce. Thankfully since then things have been a little calmer and she has towed the line.

*

Towards the end of September Frances made contact again to say that sadly both of the women turned out not to be Lena. Back to the drawing board !

My hopes were dashed again.

At the end of September Frances told me she had another lead. More waiting.

The first week of October I was told that Frances had actually spoken to Lena and Lena had written a letter for me. Frances and Margaret came to Peterborough to bring me the letter on the 14th October at 4pm.

The letter gave me some of Lena's background and education, her life to date in a loving secure family. The fact that she was married to a wonderful man and had two children. She really was shocked that I wanted contact but had told Frances that she'd thought long and hard about things and also discussed it with her mother but couldn't jeopardise her lovely close knit family.

*

So that is the story so far. I've cried rivers down the years but never so much as I have recently. I realise it must be complicated and I wouldn't want Lena to put aside her great upbringing and life as it is now but we could also offer so much. I still have a heart wrenching need to meet her one day. There always will be a chunk of my heart going to waste.

So now I can sink into a deep depression or just get on with things.

29.1.14.

To Sue Jones.

A lovely lady with a big heart. Thank you for listening to my story and your genuine sympathy.

Much love.

Helen.

x